mindful crochet

35 creative and colourful projects to help you
be in the moment, relieve stress and manage pain

emma leith

CICO BOOKS
LONDON NEW YORK

To Lili.
My fiercest critic and guiding light.

Published in 2019 by CICO Books
An imprint of Ryland Peters & Small Ltd
20–21 Jockey's Fields
London WC1R 4BW

www.rylandpeters.com

10 9 8 7 6 5 4 3

Text © Emma Leith 2019
Design, illustration, and photography
© CICO Books 2019

A CIP catalogue record for this book is
available from the British Library.

ISBN: 978 1 78249 693 9

Printed in China

Editor: Marie Clayton
Pattern checker: Jemima Bicknell
Designer: Alison Fenton
Photographer: James Gardiner
Stylist: Nel Haynes
Illustrator: Stephen Dew

Art director: Sally Powell
Production manager: Gordana Simakovic
Publishing manager: Penny Craig
Publisher: Cindy Richards

contents

introduction 6

chapter 1
colour therapy 8

mandala curtain 10
colourplay table runner 13
shisha mirrored valance 16
squares and circles stool cover 19
texture place mats 22
boho bunting 24
prayer flag garland 26
neon sunburst colour-pop bag 29
happy flowers chandelier 32

chapter 2
touch and texture 36

drifting thoughts corsage 38
mad hatter's tea cosy 40
peaceful cushion cover 43
openwork winter scarf 46
mindfulness cowl 48
meditation rug 50
ripple wrap of mindful
  imperfections 52
comfort mittens 55

chapter 3
mindful meditation 58

boho baskets 60
mandala in a hoop 63
hanging gardens plant holder 66
indian summer table mandala 68
light 'n' airy beaded toppers 71
granny love blanket 74
kaleidoscope mandala mat 77
secret garden autumn shawl 80
basketweave lap blanket 82

chapter 4
caring and sharing 84

retro flower garland 86
summer sun coasters 90
tea light holder cover 93
heart garland 96
stress ball key ring charm 99
flowers in a bobbin 102
flower power desk tidy 104
prayer beads purse 106
christmas baubles 110

techniques 112
abbreviations 127
suppliers 127
acknowledgements 127
index 128

introduction

Crochet has changed my life and I hope it will yours, too. It is the doorway to my happy place where pain and anxiety are softened and a state of peaceful acceptance resides. Crochet kept me grounded when the cancer diagnosis spun my world off its axis and it continues to help me with my pain on a daily basis. It doesn't make the bad stuff go away, but it can help transform it.

If you take one thing away from this book let it be this. Nothing is ever wasted. There is value in everything. The time spent making something that doesn't work out – a pattern gone wrong, a colour combination that doesn't hit the mark – none of this matters because it's all part of the journey and we learn something with every stitch. Our body holds on to the memory of the movement, so enjoy it all for what it is in that moment and let the hook guide you on your way. All you need to succeed with crochet is the playful desire in your heart to hook. Keep going no matter what and let the magic happen.

Happy hooking!

a note on skill levels

Each project includes a star rating as a skill level guide and listed below is an overview of the techniques needed:

- •   Easy projects requiring only basic crochet skills.
- ••   Slightly more challenging projects with repetitive stitch patterns, simple shaping or using join-as-you-go.
- •••   Advanced projects using a variety of techniques and more complex stitches.

chapter 1
colour therapy

mandala curtain

Think of each mandala as a mini-make – it can be completed in under 30 minutes and be picked up and put down anytime. If your narrative is that you're no good with colour, now's the time to change that – these colours work together in any combination, so experiment and play a little. Maybe try a colour grouping you wouldn't normally do and see how it unfolds.

SKILL RATING: ● ● ●

MATERIALS:

Rico Ricorumi DK (100% cotton, approx. 58m/63yds per 25g/⅞oz ball) DK (light worsted) weight yarn
  1 ball each of:
    Yellow shade 006
    Candy Pink shade 012
    Fuchsia shade 014
    Lilac shade 017
    Purple shade 020
    Tangerine shade 026
    Orange shade 027
    Emerald shade 042
    Light Green shade 046
    Grass Green shade 044
    Sky Blue shade 031
    Blue shade 032

3.5mm (US size E/4) and 4mm (US size G/6) crochet hooks

Yarn needle

Sewing needle and thread

FINISHED MEASUREMENTS:

Mandala: 6.5cm (2½in) diameter

Curtain: 98cm (38½in) long, 71cm (28in) wide

TENSION (GAUGE):

Exact tension is not important on this project.

ABBREVIATIONS:

See page 127.

FOR THE CURTAIN

MANDALA (make 36 – 6 per strand)

Use any sequence of colours.

Using first colour and 3.5mm (US size E/4) hook, make a magic ring, or ch6 and join with ss in first ch to form a ring.

Round 1: Ch3 (counts as first tr), 11tr into the ring, join with ss in 3rd of beg 3-ch. *12 sts.*
Fasten off.

Round 2: Join second colour in any st, ch2 (counts as 1dc and ch1), [1dc in next st, ch1] 11 times, join with ss to beg 1-ch. *12 dc + twelve 1-ch sps.*
Fasten off.

Round 3: Join third colour in any 1-ch sp, ch2 (counts as first htr), 1htr in same sp, [2htr in next 1-ch sp] to end, join with ss in 2nd of beg 2-ch. *24 sts.*
Fasten off.

Round 4: Join fourth colour in any st, ch1 (does not count as dc), [2dc in next st, 1dc in next st] 12 times. *36 sts.*
Fasten off.

BEADS (make 36 – 6 per strand – in assorted colours)

Leaving 20cm (8in) end at beg to use as stuffing for bead, using 3.5mm (US size E/4) hook, make a magic ring, or ch6 and join with ss in first ch to form a ring.

Round 1: Ch1, 6dc into the ring. Do not join, work in a continuous spiral.

Round 2: 2dc in each st around. *12 sts.*

Round 3: 1dc in each st around.

Round 4: [1dc, miss next st] 6 times. *6 sts.*

Stuff bead with beg yarn end.

Round 5: [1dc, miss next st] 3 times, join with ss in first dc.

Fasten off, thread yarn end through bead and back through again to secure.

MAKING UP AND FINISHING

For strand A, choose two strands of yarn to hold together and work as one 'chunky' strand. Thread 6 beads onto the chunky strand – do not thread the yarn through the middle of the bead but rather through one stitch only.

With both strands held together and using 4mm (US size G/6) hook, ch17, bring first bead up to the hook and ch the next stitch around it to secure, *ch25, bring the next ball up to the hook ch around the bead as before; rep until all 6 beads are secured, ch17.

Fasten off.

Make 2 more strand A.

For strand B, choose two strands of yarn to hold together and work as one 'chunky' strand. Thread 6 beads onto the chunky strand as before.

With both strands held together and using 4mm (US size G/6) hook, ch35, bring first bead up to the hook and ch the next stitch around it to secure, *ch25, bring the next ball up to the hook ch around the bead as before; rep until all 6 beads are threaded.

Fasten off.

Make 2 more strand B.

Starting from the top on the 35-ch section of strand B, use the needle and thread to sew a mandala approximately 7.5cm (3in) before the first bead. Repeat on each strand B. Sew the remaining mandalas midway on each 25-ch section between beads on all strands A and B.

Choose two strands of yarn to hold and work as one 'chunky' strand.

With both strands held together and using 4mm (US size G/6) hook, ch10, join with a ss in 10th ch from hook to form hanging loop, ch10, *join top end of strand A with 1dc, ch15, join top end of strand B with 1dc, ch15; rep until all 6 strands are joined, ch20, join with a ss in 10th ch from hook to form hanging loop.

Fasten off.

Sew in all yarn ends carefully.

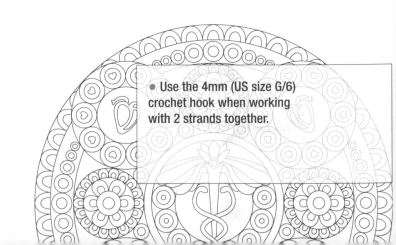

● Use the 4mm (US size G/6) crochet hook when working with 2 strands together.

colourplay table runner

The pleasure of this piece lies in how the colours go together; each works in harmony with any other, so no matter what combination you use the finished piece will be a work of beauty. I've also played with different textures and finishes – the Catona has a shiny finish that is set off beautifully alongside the soft stone washed cotton. Each yarn brings out the unique quality of the other, making this piece a real treasure.

MATERIALS:

Scheepjes Catona (100% cotton, approx. 62m/67yds per 25g/⅞oz ball) 4 ply (fingering) weight yarn

1 ball each of:
Crystalline shade 385
Powder Pink shade 238
Apple Granny shade 513
Tangerine shade 281
Delphinium shade 113
Lilac Mist shade 399
Yellow Gold shade 208

Scheepjes Stone Washed (78% cotton, 22% acrylic, approx. 130m/142yds per 50g/1¾oz ball) 5 ply (sport) weight yarn

1 ball each of:
Tourmaline shade 836
Forsterite shade 826
Amazonite shade 813
Beryl shade 833
Lilac Quartz shade 818
Rose Quartz shade 820
Pink Quartzite shade 821

4mm (US size G/6) crochet hook

Yarn needle

FINISHED MEASUREMENTS:

96.5cm (38in) long, 30.5cm (12in) wide

TENSION (GAUGE):

One square = 6cm (2¼in) square, using 4mm (US size G/6) hook.

ABBREVIATIONS:

See page 127.

FOR THE RUNNER

FOUNDATION SQUARE ROW 1

Using any colour of Catona, make a magic ring, or ch6 and join with ss in first ch to form a ring.

Round 1: Ch3 (counts as first tr), 11tr into the ring, join with ss in 3rd of beg 3-ch. *12 sts.*
Fasten off.

Round 2: Join any colour of Stone Washed in any st, ch2 (counts as first htr throughout), 1htr in same st, *2htr in each of next 2 sts, (2htr, ch2, 2htr) in next st (corner); rep from * twice, 1htr into each of next 2 sts, (2htr, ch2) into beg st, join with ss in 3rd of beg 3-ch.
Fasten off.

SECOND SQUARE ROW 1

Using any colour of Catona, make a magic ring, or ch6 and join with ss in first ch to form a ring.

Round 1: Ch3 (counts as first tr), 11tr into the ring, join with ss in 3rd of beg 3-ch. *12 sts.*
Fasten off.

Round 2: Join any colour of Stone Washed in any st, ch2, 1htr in same st, *2htr in each of next 2 sts, (2htr, ch2, 2htr) in next st (corner); rep from * twice, 1htr into each of next 2 sts, (2htr, ch1) into beg st, remove hook from loop, with RS facing throughout insert hook in any corner of foundation square, pick up loop again, pull through 2-ch corner of foundation square (joins two squares), ch1, join with ss in 3rd of beg 3-ch of second square.
Fasten off.
Make 3 more squares, joining each to prev square as set for row of 5 joined squares.

SIXTH SQUARE ROW 2

Rep second square, joining to second corner of foundation square in round 2.

ALL SUBSEQUENT SQUARES

Rep second square to end of round 1.

Round 2: Join any colour of Stone Washed in any st, ch2, 1htr in same st, 2htr in each of next 2 sts, (2htr, ch2, 2htr) in next st (2nd corner), 1htr in each of next 2 sts, (2htr, ch1) in next st, remove hook from loop, with RS facing throughout insert hook in corner of prev square in same row, pick up loop again, pull through 2-ch corner of square to join, (ch1, 2htr) in same st to complete 3rd corner, 1htr in each of next 2 sts, (2htr, ch1) in next st, removo hook from loop, with RS facing throughout insert hook in corner of matching square in prev row, pick up loop again and pull through 2-ch corner of square to join, ch1, join with ss in 3rd of beg 3-ch of original square.

This links 3 squares on 2 corners.

Cont as set until you have 16 rows of 5 squares.

Fasten off.

BORDER

Use any 2 colours of Stone Washed – I have opted for Pink Quartzite for round 1 and Tourmaline for round 2.

Round 1: Join first colour in corner sp of any side square, ch2 (counts as first htr), 1htr in same sp, miss next htr, 1htr in each of next 5 sts, miss joined corner and first htr of next square, 1htr in each of next 5 sts, (2htr, ch2, 2htr) in next corner, cont around as set, working (2htr, ch2, 2htr) in each of the two outer corner spaces of each corner square, ending with (2htr, ch2) in beg sp, join with ss in 2nd of beg 2-ch.

Fasten off.

Round 2: Join second colour in corner sp of any side square, ch1 (counts as 1dc), 1dc in same sp, *miss next htr, 1dc in each of next 5 sts, miss 3 sts, 1dc in each of next 5 sts, (2dc, ch2, 2dc) in corner sp; rep from * around, working an additional (2dc, ch2, 2dc) in the second outer corner of each corner square, ending with (2dc, ch2) in beg sp, join with ss in beg 1-ch.

Fasten off.

MAKING UP AND FINISHING

Sew in all yarn ends carefully.

This piece will need to be blocked to ensure it lays flat and looks its best.

MINDFULNESS

Notice if there is a certain colour combination that you gravitate toward and whether this changes depending upon how you are feeling – do your spirits lift or thought patterns change as your colour combinations emerge from the hook?

shisha mirrored valance

Having a blast of happiness that frames your doorway or window can sometimes be just the tonic on those gloomy days. I love working with these little mirrors and enjoy seeing the light reflect and bounce around the room, adding sparkle to the crochet. This piece is designed to be worked in stages, making small elements that are joined together at the end, so this is a 'pick up and put down' project.

MINDFULNESS

These colours all work together in any combination so be inspired by what you see and follow your heart. You may decide to go heavy on the blues and greens, which will result in a cooler feel to the finished piece but will be just as cheery. Let the colours work their magic as you crochet your squares, and notice the effects they have on your thoughts and mood.

SKILL RATING: ● ● ○

MATERIALS:

For the valance:
Scheepjes Catona (100% cotton, approx. 62.5m/68yds per 25g/⁷⁄₈oz ball) 4 ply (fingering) weight yarn
1 ball each of:
Shocking Pink shade 114
Fresia shade 519
Lavender shade 520
Tangerine shade 281
Yellow Gold shade 208
Lime Juice shade 392
Jade shade 514
Cyan shade 397
Electric Blue shade 201

Scheepjes Catona (100% cotton, approx. 125m/136yds per 50g/1¾oz ball) 4 ply (fingering) weight yarn
1 ball of Bridal White shade 105

3.75mm (US size F/5) crochet hook

Yarn needle

81 small glass beads

For the mirror frames:
Scheepjes Maxi Sweet Treat (100% cotton, approx. 140m/153yds per 25g/⁷⁄₈oz ball) lace weight yarn
1 ball each of:
Cyan shade 397
Electric Blue shade 201
Vivid Blue shade 146
Jade shade 514

2mm (US size B/1) crochet hook

34 shisha mirrors

FINISHED MEASUREMENTS:
81cm (32in) long, 23cm (9in) deep

TENSION (GAUGE):
19 sts x 24 rows = 10cm (4in) over double crochet, using 3.75mm (US size F/5) hook and Scheepjes Catona.

ABBREVIATIONS:
See page 127.

SPECIAL ABBREVIATION:
bead picot: ch1, bring bead to hook, ch1 around bead, ch1, ss in first ch

FOR THE VALANCE
SQUARES (MAKE 8)
Using first colour and 3.75mm (US size F/5) hook, make a magic ring, or ch6 and join with ss in first ch to form a ring.
Round 1: Ch2 (counts as first htr throughout), 11htr into the ring, join with ss in 2nd of beg 2-ch. *12 sts.*
Round 2: Ch2, 1htr in same st, 2htr in each st to end, join with ss in 2nd of beg 2-ch. *24 sts.* Fasten off first colour.
Round 3: Join second colour in any st, ch2, (1htr, ch2, 2htr) in same st as join (corner), *1htr in each of next 5 sts, (2htr, ch2, 2htr) in next st (corner); rep from * twice, 1htr in each of next 5 sts, join with ss in 2nd of beg 2-ch. *36 sts + four 2-ch sps.* Fasten off second colour.
Round 4: Join third colour in any corner 2-ch sp, ch1 (counts as first dc throughout), (1dc, ch2, 2dc) in same sp as join, *miss next st, 1dc in each of next 8 sts, (2dc, ch2, 2dc) in next corner 2-ch sp; rep from * twice, miss next st, 1dc in each of next 8 sts, join with ss in beg 1-ch. *48 sts + four 2-ch sps.* Fasten off third colour.
Round 5: Join fourth colour in any corner 2-ch sp, ch1, (1dc, ch2, 2dc) in same sp as join, *miss next st, 1dc in each of next 11 sts, (2dc, ch2, 2dc) in next corner 2-ch sp; rep from twice, miss next st, 1dc in each of next 11 sts, join with ss in beg 1-ch. *60 sts + four 2-ch sps.* Fasten off fourth colour.

- The shisha mirrors are available online.
- To fix the valance to either a door or window frame, sew the soft half of a strip of Velcro to the WS of the top band. Then attach the rough half of the Velcro to the surface from which you wish to hang your crochet.

Round 6: Join fifth colour in any corner 2-ch sp, ch2, (1htr, ch2, 2htr) in same sp as join, *miss next st, 1htr in each of next 14 sts, (2htr, ch2, 2htr) in next corner 2-ch sp; rep from * twice, miss next st, 1htr in each of next 14 sts, join with ss in 2nd of beg 2-ch. *72 sts + four 2-ch sps.* Fasten off.

TRIANGLE FLAG (MAKE 8)
Take any square and with RS facing and using 3.75mm (US size F/5) hook, join yarn into any 2-ch sp corner.
Row 1: Ch1 (counts as first dc), 1dc in each of next 18 sts. *19 sts.*

Row 2: Turn, ch1 (does not count as st), miss first st, 1dc in each st to last 2 sts, dc2tog. *17 sts.*
Rows 3–10: Rep row 2. *1 st.*
Fasten off.

MAKING UP AND FINISHING

Lay the squares down in a line in any sequence you like, with their triangle flags at the bottom. Using the yarn needle and matching yarn, and with squares RS tog, join the squares into a strip using whip stitch (see page 125). Do not join the triangle flags.

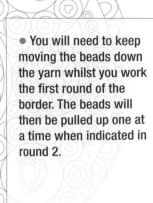

● You will need to keep moving the beads down the yarn whilst you work the first round of the border. The beads will then be pulled up one at a time when indicated in round 2.

WHITE BEADED BORDER

Thread 81 glass beads onto Bridal White, push down until needed. With RS facing and using 3.75mm (US size F/5) hook, join yarn at top right corner sp of crochet strip.

Round 1: Ch1 (counts as 1dc throughout), 1dc in each st along top edge to corner working 1dc into each square join (152 sts), (1dc, ch1, 1dc) in corner sp, miss next st of square, 1dc in each of next 17 sts along side edge of square, *1dc in each row end to tip of triangle (9 sts), (1dc, ch1, 1dc) in tip of triangle, 1dc in each row end to top of triangle (9 sts); rep from * on all triangles, 1dc in each of next 17 sts along side edge of square, ch1, join with ss in beg 1-ch.

Round 2 (beaded round): Ch1, 1dc in each st along top edge to corner sp, (1dc, ch1, 1dc) in corner sp, 1dc in each of next 17 sts, *[bead picot, 1dc in each of next 2 sts] 4 times, bead picot, 1dc in next st, (1dc, bead picot, 1dc) in tip of triangle, [1dc in each of next 2 sts, bead picot] 4 times, 1dc in each of next 3 sts (3rd dc is in st joining two triangles); rep from * along all triangles, bead picot, 1dc in each of next 17 sts along side edge of square, (1dc, ch1) in beg corner, join with ss into beg 1-ch.

Do not fasten off.

TOP BAND

Row 1: Ch1 (counts as first dc), ch1, miss next st, *1dc, ch1, miss next st; rep from * to last st, 1dc in last st, changing to next colour on last dc.

Row 2: Ch2, [1dc in next 1-ch sp, ch1, miss next st] to end, 1dc in last 1-ch sp, changing to next colour on last dc.

Rows 3–9: Rep rows 1 and 2, changing colour on each row.

Rows 10–12: Using one colour only, ch1, 1dc in each st and sp to end.

Fasten off.

SINGLE MIRROR FRAMES (MAKE 26)

Using any Maxi Sweet Treat yarn and 2mm (US size B/1) hook, make a magic ring.

Round 1: Ch1 (does not count as st throughout), 24dc into the ring, ss in first dc. *24 sts.*

Fasten off first colour. Pull yarn end to tighten ring but leave enough space to view mirror through.

Round 2: Join second colour, ch1, [2dc in next st, 1dc in each of next 5 sts] 4 times, ss in first dc to join. *28 sts.*

Fasten off.

Position the frame in place on the main panel of squares and oversew (see page 124) halfway around using the round 2 colour. Slide the mirror under the frame and finish sewing the frame to the panel.

DOUBLE MIRROR FRAMES (MAKE 8)

To make the double-sided mirror frames to hang underneath each triangle, make 16 single frames as above (2 for each mirror). Place with WS together, matching stitches around the edge, and join with a double crochet seam (see page 124), working 2dc in every seventh stitch and using yarn to match round 2. Insert two mirrors back to back into frame when about halfway around, then complete the seam and join with a ss in the first dc.

Fasten off, leaving a 20cm (8in) end. Sew the double-sided mirror into the stitch at the peak of each triangle in round 2 of the beaded border.

Sew in all yarn ends carefully.

squares and circles stool cover

This cover is designed to fit a square stool. I like to sit and make all the colourful circles first. If you are new to the join-as-you-go method, then I recommend you sit quietly with no distractions whilst you practise this simple technique of joining two squares as you crochet the side. Essentially you are slip stitching two squares together between each three-treble cluster, instead of making the chain.

SKILL RATING: ● ● ○

MATERIALS:

Rico Creative Cotton Aran (100% cotton, approx. 85m/92yds per 50g/1¾oz ball) Aran (worsted) weight yarn
  1 ball each of:
    Natural shade 60 (MC)
    Candy Pink shade 64
    Tangerine shade 76
    Banana shade 68
    Violet shade 16
    Sky Blue shade 37
    Light Green shade 40
    Light Pistachio shade 44

4.5mm (US size 7) crochet hook

Yarn needle

FINISHED MEASUREMENTS:

To fit a 33cm (13in) square stool

TENSION (GAUGE):

Rounds 1–2 of 3-colour circle = 6.5cm (2½in) diameter, using 4.5mm (US size 7) hook.

ABBREVIATIONS:

See page 127.

FOR THE COVER

3-COLOUR CIRCLES (make 9)

Using first colour, make a magic ring, or ch6 and join with ss in first ch to form a ring.

Round 1: Ch3 (counts as first tr throughout), 11tr into the ring, join with ss in 3rd of beg 3-ch. *12 sts.*

Fasten off first colour.

Round 2: Join second colour in any st, ch3, 1tr in same st, [2tr in each st] to end, join with ss in 3rd of beg 3-ch. *24 sts.*

Fasten off second colour.

Round 3: Join third colour in any st, ch3, 1tr in same st, 1tr in next st, [2tr in next st, 1tr in next st] 11 times, join with ss in 3rd of beg 3-ch. *36 sts.*

Fasten off third colour.

Lay out circles in 3 rows of 3 in desired order.

When turning circles into squares you will join each square from left to right.

FIRST LARGE SQUARE

Round 4: Join MC in any st of any circle, ch3 (counts as first tr), 2tr in same st, ch1, *miss 2 sts, 3htr in next st, ch1, miss 2 sts, 3htr in next st, ch1, miss 2 sts, (3tr, ch2, 3tr) in next st (corner); rep from * twice, miss 2 sts, 3htr in next st, ch1, miss 2 sts, 3htr in next st, ch1, miss 2 sts, (3tr, ch2) in beg st (fourth corner), join with ss in 3rd of beg 3-ch.

Fasten off.

JOINING LARGE SQUARES

Round 4: Join MC in any st of next circle, ch3 (counts as first tr), 2tr in same st, ch1, miss 2 sts, 3htr in next st, ch1, miss 2 sts, 3htr in next st, ch1, miss 2 sts, 3tr in next st, join with ss in corresponding corner of starting square by inserting hook in corner sp of starting square from underneath, 1dc in corner sp of starting square (counts as first of 2-ch for corner sp), ch1, work 3tr in same st of current square as prev 3-tr to complete corner. Cont to join squares tog with 1dc in next side sp of starting square, 3tr in next side sp of current square. Cont replacing each 1-ch at sides of current square with 1dc in next side sp of starting square to next corner and then replace first of 2-ch at corner sp of current square with 1dc in corner sp of starting square to finish joining the side. Complete the current square as normal, following round 4 of first large square above.

When joining a square to 2 prev squares, replace both corner ch of current square with 1dc in each adjoining square. Cont working join-as-you-go method (see page 122) to make one large panel of 3 by 3 squares.

SMALL SIDE SQUARES (make 24)

Using any colour, make a magic ring, or ch6 and join with ss in first ch to form a ring.

Round 1: Ch3 (counts as first tr throughout), 11tr into the ring, join with ss in 3rd of beg 3-ch. *12 sts.*
Fasten off first colour.

Round 2: Join MC in any st, ch3, 2tr in same st, miss 2 sts, (3tr, ch2, 3tr) in next st (corner), miss 2 sts, 3tr in next st, using join-as you-go method as above, starting in any corner of main panel, join with 1dc onto corner sp of first large square on main panel, ch1, 3tr in same st as prev 3-tr, join with 1dc onto next side sp of main panel square, miss 2 sts, 3tr in next st, join with 1dc onto next sp of main panel square, ch1, 3tr in same st as prev 3-tr, miss next 2 sts, (3tr, ch2) in beg st (fourth corner), join with ss in 3rd of beg 3-ch.

Cont to join squares on round 2 in this way, make and join 2 small side squares to each large square (6 small squares per side). After working the first square on each side, join each subsequent square in this way to one side of the prev small square, as well as the main panel square.
Fasten off.

MINI CIRCLES FOR BORDER (make 24)

Using any colour, make a magic ring, or ch6 and join with ss in first ch to form a ring.

Round 1: Ch1 (counts as first dc throughout), 7dc into the ring, join with ss in beg 1-ch. *8 sts.*
Fasten off first colour.

Round 2: Join second colour in any st, ch1, 1dc in same st, 2dc in each st to end, join with ss in beg 1-ch. *16 sts.*
Fasten off, leaving 10cm (4in) end.

MAKING UP AND FINISHING

Oversew (see page 124) the sides of the two adjoining small squares together at each corner to bring the sides down to form the stool top shape.

BOTTOM EDGING

Round 1: Join MC in right-hand corner sp of any small square, ch1 (counts as first dc), *miss next st, 1dc in each of next 5 sts, 1dc in corner sp of square, 1dc in corner sp of next square; rep from * to last square, miss next st, 1dc in each of next 5 sts, 1dc in corner sp of last square, join with ss in beg 1-ch.

Round 2: Ch1, [1dc in each of next 5 sts, dc2tog] 24 times.
Fasten off.

Thread the yarn end of a mini circle onto the yarn needle and sew to hang at the base of the cover at one corner. Repeat at each corner, then add five more evenly spaced along each side.

Fasten off and sew in all yarn ends carefully.

texture place mats

These mats are made with one of my all time favourite stitches, and when worked with two strands of yarn held together the density and woven texture is amplified – making this the perfect stitch for place mats. The beauty of this pattern is that once the foundation row is established you will be working in the chain spaces throughout, making it a smooth and restful crochet experience.

SKILL RATING: ● ● ●

MATERIALS:

Rico Creative Cotton Aran (100% cotton, approx. 85m/92yds per 50g/1¾oz ball) Aran (worsted) weight yarn
1 ball each of:
  Natural shade 60
  Rose shade 00
  Candy Pink shade 64
  Fuchsia shade 13
  Light Blue shade 32
  Sky Blue shade 37
  Light Green shade 40
  Light Pistachio shade 44
  Banana shade 68
  Tangerine shade 76
  Orange shade 74

6mm (US size J/10) crochet hook

Yarn needle

FINISHED MEASUREMENTS:

24cm (9½in) wide, 21cm (8¼in) long

TENSION (GAUGE):

15 sts x 14 rows = 10cm (4in) over patt, using 6mm (US size J/10) hook and two strands of yarn held together.

ABBREVIATIONS:

See page 127.

FOR THE PLACE MATS

Hold two strands of different colours tog throughout.
Using any two colours held tog, ch38.
Row 1: 1dc in 4th ch from hook, *ch1, miss next st, 1dc in foll st; rep from * to end, changing to next 2 colours on last dc, turn. *18 dc + eighteen 1-ch sps.*
Row 2: Ch2 (counts as 1 ch sp), 1dc in first 1-ch sp, *ch1, 1dc in next 1-ch sp; rep from * to end, changing to next 2 colours on last dc, turn.
Rep row 1 until 31 rows have been worked.
Fasten off, leaving 15cm (6in) ends.

MAKING UP AND FINISHING

To secure the yarn ends, gather the four strands per row together and tie in a double knot. Lay the mat flat and trim the ends to make a 2.5cm (1in) long fringe on each side.

- Adjust the size to suit your plates – but always start with an even number of chain.

- Change colour on each row on the last yarn round hook of the current row. Leave 15cm (6in) yarn ends when joining and fastening off to make the fringe later.

- To create a subtle pattern that pleases the eye without being noticeably obvious, work every third row with a cream and a pastel shade held together.

boho bunting

Lift the spirits with this gloriously happy bunting, featuring colours that ping and pop against the contrast of bold black and white. The magic of this project is in the colour, so note how each colour makes you feel. Does the use of black and white alter your response to a particular colour? As you focus your mind toward the interplay of colours can you begin to see preferences and patterns emerging?

MINDFULNESS

Each triangle can be completed in a half-hour sitting and there's no rush. This project requires a little bit of counting on each round, so practise making the counting slow and rhythmical. Slowing the stitches slows the mind and the breath.

SKILL RATING: ● ● ●

MATERIALS:

Scheepjes Cahlista (100% cotton, approx. 85m/92yds per 50g/1¾oz ball) Aran (worsted) weight yarn

1 ball each of:
- Jet Black shade 110 (A)
- Bridal White shade 105 (B)
- Shocking Pink shade 114
- Tulip shade 222
- Lemon shade 280
- Yellow Gold shade 208
- Tangerine shade 281
- Apple Granny shade 513
- Cyan shade 397
- Delphinium shade 113

4.5mm (US size 7) crochet hook

Yarn needle

FINISHED MEASUREMENTS:

Bunting: 175cm (69in) long, 16.5cm (6½in) deep

TENSION (GAUGE):

Rounds 1–3 = 7cm (2¾in) diameter, using 4.5mm (US size 7) hook.

ABBREVIATIONS:

See page 127.

SPECIAL ABBREVIATION:

edc (elongated double crochet): insert hook in st two rows below current row, yrh, pull yarn up level to current row, yrh, pull through both loops on hook to complete edc

FOR THE BUNTING

TRIANGLES (make 7)

Using the first colour, make a magic ring, or ch6 and join with ss in first ch to form a ring.

Round 1: Ch3 (counts as first tr throughout), 11tr into the ring, join with ss in 3rd of beg 3-ch. *12 sts.*
Fasten off first colour.

Round 2: Join A in any st, ch2 (counts as first htr), 1htr in same st, [2htr in next st] 11 times, join with ss in 2nd of beg 2-ch. *24 sts.*
Fasten off A.

Round 3: Join B in any st from row 1, pull yarn up to current row and ch1 (counts as first edc), [1dc in next st, 1edc in next st] 11 times, join with ss in first edc. *12 dc + 12 edc.*
Fasten off.

Round 4: Join second colour in any st, ch1 (counts as first dc), [ch2, miss next st, 1dc in foll st] 11 times, ch2, miss last st, join with ss in beg 1-ch. *12 dc + twelve 2-ch sps.*
Fasten off second colour.

Round 5: Join third colour in any 2-ch sp, ch3, 2tr in same sp, [3htr in next 2-ch sp] 3 times, (3tr, ch2, 3tr) in next sp (first corner), [3htr in next 2-ch sp] 3 times, (3tr, ch2, 3tr) in next sp (second corner), [3htr in next 2-ch sp] 3 times, 3tr into beg 2-ch sp, ch2, join with ss in 3rd of beg 3-ch (third corner).
Fasten off.

Round 6: Join B in any corner 2-ch sp, ch1 (counts as first dc), [ch3, miss next 2 sts, 1dc in foll st] 4 times, ch3, (1dc, ch2, 1dc) in next corner 2-ch sp, [ch3, miss next 2 sts, 1dc in foll st] 4 times, ch3, (1dc, ch2, 1dc) in next corner 2-ch sp, [ch3, miss next 2 sts, 1dc in foll st] 4 times, ch3, 1dc in beg 2-ch sp, ch2, join with ss in beg 1-ch.
Fasten off B.

Round 7: Join fourth colour in any corner 2-ch sp, ch1 (counts as first dc), *[(1dc, 2htr, 1dc) in next 2-ch sp] 5 times, (1dc, 1htr, ch1, 1htr, 1dc) in next corner 2-ch sp; rep from * once more, [(1dc, 2htr, 1dc) in next 2-ch sp] 5 times, (1dc, 1htr, ch1, 1htr) in beg corner 2-ch sp, join with ss in beg 1-ch.
Fasten off fourth colour.

MAKING UP AND FINISHING

Sew in all yarn ends carefully.

JOIN THE TRIANGLES

Row 1: Using B, ch15, join with ss to beg ch to form hanging loop, ch10, *with triangle RS facing, 1tr in any 2-ch sp corner, [ch3, miss next 3 sts, 1dc in foll st] 5 times, ch3, 1tr in next 2-ch sp corner, ch5; rep from * until all 7 triangles are joined, ch25, join with ss in 15th ch from hook to form hanging loop.

Row 2: Ch1 (does not count as st throughout), 1dc in each st and ch to start of beg hanging loop.
Fasten off B.

Row 3: Join A in first dc, ch1, 1dc in each st to end.
Fasten off A.

Row 4: Join B in first dc, ch1, *1dc, 1edc in next st from row 1; rep from * to end.
Fasten off and sew in yarn ends.

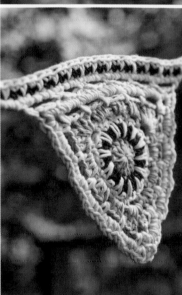

● Mix and match the colours to suit your mood whilst following this simple colour pattern: row 2 is always black, rows 3 and 6 are always white. Everything else is up to you – just remember to change colour with every round!

● Cotton holds its shape well, making it perfect for bunting, but as always with Aran (worsted) cotton take it slow because the yarn can split and there's not a lot of springy softness to it.

prayer flag garland

This is the ultimate stash buster project where anything goes! Once completed these prayer flags are small enough to be hung just about anywhere and will bring a little happiness wherever they are. Making colourful crochet pieces to decorate and adorn your living space can have a positive impact on your mental health. These crochet creations are imbued with the pleasure associated with crochet and give meaning and value as well as sparkles of colour to your home.

SKILL RATING: ● ● ●

MATERIALS:

Rico Ricorumi DK (100% cotton, approx. 57m/62yds per 25g/⅞oz ball) DK (light worsted) weight yarn
Small amount each of:
Cream shade 002 (A)
Orange shade 027 (B)
Fuchsia shade 014 (C)
Sky Blue shade 031
Grass Green shade 044
Blue shade 032
Light Green shade 046
Tangerine shade 026
Yellow shade 006
Lilac shade 017

Rico Essentials Cotton DK (100% cotton, approx. 130m/142yds per 50g/1¾oz ball) DK (light worsted) weight yarn
Small amount each of:
Violet shade 20
Aquamarine shade 31
Pistachio shade 86

Rico Fashion Cotton Metallise (53% cotton, 35% acrylic, 12% metallic, approx. 130m/142yds per 50g/1¾oz ball) DK (light worsted) weight yarn
Small amount of:
Silver shade 004

4mm (US size G/6) crochet hook

Yarn needle

FINISHED MEASUREMENTS:

100cm (39½in) long

TENSION (GAUGE):

Each flag = 7cm (2¾in) wide, 9cm (3½in) long, using 4mm (US size G/6) hook.

ABBREVIATIONS:

See page 127.

SPECIAL ABBREVIATION:

edc (elongated double crochet): insert hook in st two rows below current row, yrh, pull yarn up level to current row, yrh, pull through both loops on hook to complete edc

FOR THE GARLAND

FLAGS (make 7)

When changing colour, introduce new colour on last yrh of final st of current row and leave 15cm (6in) ends. Work over both yarn ends when working next row, except as indicated.

Using any colour, ch14.

Row 1: 1htr in 3rd ch from hook, 1htr in each ch to end, changing to next colour on last st, turn. *12 sts.*

Row 2: Ch2 (does not count as st throughout), 1htr in each st to end, changing to next colour on last st, turn.

Do not work over both yarn ends when working row 3.

Row 3: Ch3 (does not count as a st), miss st at base of ch, 1htr in next st, [ch1, miss next st, 1htr in foll st] 5 times, changing to next colour on last st, turn.

Row 4: Ch2, 2htr in each 1-ch sp from prev row ending with 2htr in last sp between beg 3-ch and htr from prev row, changing to next colour on last st, turn.

Row 5: Ch1 (does not count as st throughout), 1dc in each st to end, changing to next colour on last st, turn. *12 sts.*

Row 6: Ch1, [1dc, 1edc] to end, changing to next colour on last st, turn. *6 dc + 6 edc.*

Do not work over both yarn ends when working row 7.

Row 7: Rep row 3.
Row 8: Rep row 4.
Row 9: Rep row 5.
Row 10: Rep row 2.
Row 11: Rep row 5.
Fasten off.

MAKING UP AND FINISHING

Sew in all yarn ends from rows 2 and 7. For the ends that have been worked over there should be little ends poking out the other end of the row. Gently pull to tighten up the flag and cut off the excess end.

JOIN THE FLAGS

Using A, ch15, join with ss in beg ch to make first hanging loop, ch10, *with RS facing, 1dc in each st along top edge of flag (12 sts), ch10; rep from * until all 7 flags are joined, ending last rep with ch25, join with ss in 15th ch to make second hanging loop,
Next row: Ch1, 1dc in each st and ch to to beg of first hanging loop.
Fasten off.

Cut a length of B and C, each 30cm (12in) longer than the length of the garland just made. With both strands in a yarn needle, thread through one end of the garland and secure with a knot. Weave in and out of each dc of the garland to the other end.
Fasten off.

Sew in all yarn ends carefully.

ADD THE TASSELS

Cut lengths of each colour approx. 6.5cm (2½in) long. Holding one strand of two colours together, make a tassel (see page 125). Attach one tassel to the first and last stitches of the bottom edge of a flag, and space another four tassels equally between them. Repeat for the other flags. Trim the tassels to the desired length.

• Work any DK (light worsted) yarn you have, in any colour combination – I changed colour for each row. Keeping these flags small means you can use up all those little scraps of yarn, making it no big deal to experiment with colour and just pull out a row if you don't like the result.

• The pattern can be adapted to make larger flags by simply increasing the foundation chain in multiples of two.

neon sunburst colour-pop bag

The colours in this project are designed to wake up your senses and elevate your playful spirit! This is a great stashbuster project – you can use up all those scraps of yarn left over from other makes.

MATERIALS:

Stylecraft Special DK (100% acrylic, approx. 295m/322yds per 100g/3½oz ball) DK (light worsted) weight yarn

1 ball each of:
Black shade 1002 (A)
Cream shade 1005 (B)
Bright Green shade 1259
Sherbet shade 1034
Aspen shade 1422
Cloud Blue shade 1019
Turquoise shade 1068
Bluebell shade 1082
Lobelia shade 1825
Wisteria shade 1432
Violet shade 1277
Lipstick shade 1246
Fiesta shade 1257
Jaffa shade 1256
Sunshine shade 1114
Spring Green shade 1316
Candyfloss shade 1130
Saffron shade 1081
Fondant shade 1241

Rico Fashion Cotton Metallise (53% cotton, 35% acrylic, 12% metallic, approx. 130m/142yds per 50g/1¾oz ball) DK (light worsted) weight yarn

1 ball each of:
Gold shade 003
Silver shade 004

4mm (US size G/6) crochet hook

Yarn needle

Jute bag or similar

Sewing needle and thread

3.5cm (1⅜in) pompom maker

1 large wooden bead per tassel

1 key ring hook per tassel

FINISHED MEASUREMENTS:

30 x 30 x 18cm (12 x 12 x 7¼in)

TENSION (GAUGE):

Five 3-tr groups x 9 rows = 10cm (4in) square over patt, using 4mm (US size G/6) hook.

ABBREVIATIONS:

See page 127.

FOR THE BAG

SQUARE CENTRE (make 2)

Using any colour, ch6 and join with ss in first ch to form a ring.

Round 1: Ch3 (counts as first tr throughout), 2tr into ring, *ch3, 3tr in ring; rep from * twice more, join with ss in 3rd of beg 3-ch.
Fasten off first colour.

Round 2: Join second colour in any corner 3-ch sp, ch3, 2tr in same 3-ch sp (half corner made), *ch1, (3tr, ch2, 3tr) in next 3-ch sp (corner made); rep from * twice more (changing to third colour halfway through 3rd corner), ch1, 3tr in same sp as beg half corner, ch2, join with ss in 3rd of beg 3-ch.
Fasten off.

Round 3: Join fourth colour in any corner 2-ch sp, ch3, 2tr in same 2-ch sp (half corner made), *ch1, 3tr in next 1-ch sp, ch1, (3tr, ch2, 3tr) in next 2-ch sp (corner made); rep from * twice more (changing to fifth colour halfway through 3rd corner), ch1, 3tr in next 1-ch sp, ch1, 3tr in same sp as beg half corner, ch2, join with ss in 3rd of beg 3-ch.
Fasten off.

FRONT AND BACK SQUARES (make 2)

Rounds 4–12: Cont to work patt as in round 3, changing colour as desired, working 3tr in each 1-ch sp, separated by 1-ch, and (3tr, ch2, 3tr) in each corner 2-ch sp.

Round 13: Join A in any corner 2-ch sp, ch1 (counts as first dc throughout), [1dc in each st and 1-ch sp to next corner 2-ch sp, (1dc, ch2, 1dc) in corner 2-ch sp] 3 times, 1dc in each st and 1-ch sp to beg corner 2-ch sp, 1dc in corner 2-ch sp, ch2, join with ss in beg 1-ch and change to B.

Round 14: Using B, ch1, [1dc in each st to next corner 2-ch sp, (1dc, ch2, 1dc) in corner 2-ch sp] 3 times, 1dc in each st to beg corner 2-ch sp, 1dc in corner 2-ch sp, ch2, join with ss in beg 1-ch and change to A.
Fasten off B.

Round 15: Using A, rep row 14.
Fasten off.

 • For a larger bag, work additional rounds after round 3 on the centre.

SIDE PANELS (make 3)

You'll work and join squares for sides and base using join-as-you-go method (see page 122).

Make 1 square (starter square A) by working rounds 1–5 as above.
Make 1 square (side square B) by working rounds 1–4 as above.

Join side square B to the starter square A working join-as-you-go method as foll:

Round 5: Ch3, 2tr in same 2-ch sp (half corner made), ch1, (3tr, ch1) in each 1-ch sp to next corner 2-ch sp, 3tr in corner 2-ch sp. Then, instead of making ch2 for corner sp, insert hook in corner sp of starter square from underneath, 1dc in corner 2-ch sp of starter square (counts as first of 2-ch for corner sp), ch1, 3tr in corner 2-ch sp of second square to complete the corner.

To cont joining squares, instead of ch1 work 1dc in next side sp of starter square, 3tr in next side sp of second square. Cont replacing each ch1 at side of second square with 1dc in next side sp of starting square, and replacing first of ch2 at corner sp of current square with 1dc in corner sp of starter square. When second square has been joined to starting square along one side, cont around to finish final round of current square as normal.
Fasten off.

Round 6: Cont to work patt as in round 3, working around entire edge of side panel and treating the 'corner' spaces on each side of join as 1-ch sps.
Fasten off.
Round 7: Using A, rep round 13 of front and back squares.
Round 8: Using B, rep round 14 of front and back squares.
Round 9: Using A, rep round 15 of front and back squares.
This makes one side panel. Make 3 more side panels.

MAKING UP AND FINISHING

Sew in all yarn ends carefully.

JOIN SIDES TO FRONT AND BACK

Align one large square and one side panel with WS together. Join any colour yarn in corner 2-ch sp of both squares and work a double crochet seam (see page 124). Fasten off.
Rep to add the other 2 side panels, then join the ends of the side panels.

Add the other large square on the other edge of the side panels to complete the bag.

Place the jute bag inside the crochet bag and sew whip stitch (see page 125) around the top edge to secure in place.

POMPOM TASSEL

Make 4 pompoms (see page 125), leaving 30cm (12in) ends. Using any combination of yarn colours, wrap yarn thickly around a 10cm (4in) piece of card. Cut a 25cm (10in) length of yarn, slide it under the strands and tie in a knot at the top. Remove the tassel from the card, and bind it securely just below the top, using a contrasting colour of yarn.

Thread beads onto the end at the top of a tassel, add the first pompom, thread on more beads, then add the second pompom. Secure the yarn end to a key ring hook. Repeat for the second tassel, then clip both to one side of the bag.

happy flowers chandelier This colourful

hanging decoration will really brighten up any room. Let this project take you on a little journey toward a happier way of being. One small circle can be made in minutes so there's no need to rush.

SKILL RATING: ● ● ●

MATERIALS:

For the chandelier:
Scheepjes Cahlista (100% cotton, approx. 85m/92yds per 50g/1¾oz ball) Aran (worsted) weight yarn
  1 ball each of:
    Bridal White shade 105 (A)
    Jet Black shade 110 (B)
    Apple Granny shade 513
    Lemon shade 280
    Cyan shade 397
    Crystalline shade 385
    Bluebird shade 247
    Shocking Pink shade 114
    Tangerine shade 281
    Royal Orange shade 189
    Lavender shade 520

Scheepjes Catona (100% cotton, approx. 25m/27yds per 10g/⅜oz ball) 4 ply (fingering) weight yarn
  1 ball each of:
    Lemon shade 280
    Icy Pink shade 246
    Sweet Orange shade 411
    Shocking Pink shade 114

Cyan shade 397
    Apple Granny shade 513
    Lavender shade 520
    Lilac Mist shade 399

Twilleys Goldfingering (80% viscose, 20% polyester, approx. 100m/109yds per 25g/⅞oz ball) 4 ply (fingering) weight yarn
  1 x ball of Antique Gold shade 004

For the pompoms:
Stylecraft Special DK (100% acrylic, approx. 295m/322yds per 100g/3½oz ball) DK (light worsted) weight yarn
  1 x ball of Cream shade 1005

4mm (US size G/6) crochet hook

Stitch marker

Yarn needle

Polyester toy filling

25cm (10in) inner embroidery hoop (part without metal fastening)

3.5cm (1⅜in) and 5.5cm (2¼in) pompom makers

FINISHED MEASUREMENTS:

Approx. 81cm (32in) total hanging depth, 25cm (10in) diameter

TENSION (GAUGE):

One mini disc = 3cm (1¼in) diameter, using 4mm (US size G/6) hook.

ABBREVIATIONS:

See page 127.

FOR THE CHANDELIER

MINI DISCS (make 95 in total – 40 for top, 45 for bottom)
Using any colour of Cahlista, make a magic ring, or ch6 and join with ss in first ch to form a ring.
Round 1: Ch3 (counts as first tr), 11tr into ring, join with ss in 3rd of beg 3-ch. *12 sts.*
Fasten off and sew in ends.

BALLS (make 15 in total: 10 for top, 5 for bottom)
Using any colour of Cahlista, make a magic ring, or ch4 and join with ss in first ch to form a ring.
Round 1: Ch1 (does not count as st), 6dc into the ring. *6 sts.*
Work in a continuous spiral. PM in last st and move up as each round is finished.
Round 2: 2dc in each st to end. *12 sts.*
Rounds 3 and 4: 1dc in each st to end.
Keep RS facing as the edge begins to curve up.
Round 5: [1dc in next st, dc2tog] 4 times. *8 sts.*
Insert toy filling.
Round 6: [Dc2tog] 4 times. *4 sts.*
Fasten off leaving a 10cm (4in) end, draw end through all rem sts and pull tight.

FLOWERS (make 10)
Using B, make a magic ring, or ch6 and join with ss in first ch to form a ring.
Round 1: Ch3 (counts as first tr), 9tr into the ring, join with ss in 3rd of beg 3-ch. *10 sts.*
Round 2: Using any colour of Cahlista and Goldfingering held together as one strand, join yarn in any st, ch4 (counts as first dc and ch3), miss next st, [1dc in next st, ch3, miss next st] 4 times, join with ss in first of beg 4-ch. *5dc + five 3-ch sps.*
Fasten off.
Round 3: Using any colour of Cahlista and Catona held together as one strand, join yarn in any 3-ch sp, *ch4, (3dtr, ch4, ss) in next 3-ch sp (petal made); rep from * 4 more times. *5 petals.*
Fasten off.

MAKING UP AND FINISHING

Sew in all yarn ends carefully.

SUSPENDING STRINGS (make 5)

Cut a 240cm (96in) length each of A and B, hold them together and thread onto a yarn needle.

Work with both yarns as one strand and leaving 20cm (8in) at the end without the yarn needle, ch6. Fasten off to create a knot. Fasten off to create a knot after every section of ch as you continue.

Thread the yarns through the centre of 1 ball, then bring the ball down to sit on top of the length of chain. Ch6, thread the yarns through the centre of 1 disc, bring the disc down to sit on top of the length of ch. Ch2, thread on a second disc, ch2, thread on a third disc.

Ch6, thread on a second ball, ch6, thread on a fourth disc, [ch2, thread on a disc] 4 times.

Fasten off, leaving a 40cm (16in) end.

POMPOMS

Using A, make five 3.5cm (1⅜in) pompoms and one 5.5cm (2¼in) pompom.

ASSEMBLING THE TOP

Using the 20cm (8in) yarn end, tie each suspending string to the wooden hoop ensuring they are evenly spaced around. Hold all the strings together at the top and adjust so the ring is evenly balanced when it hangs. Tie the ends together in one large knot.

At the top there are now 10 strands (5 in A, 5 in B). Cut off 8 strands above the large knot, leaving 1 in A and 1 in B. Thread the 5.5cm (2¼in) pompom onto these and bring the pompom down to just above the large knot. Using the 2 remaining strands, ch20, ss in first ch to make a loop to suspend the chandelier.

BOTTOM STRINGS (make 10)

Cut a 70cm (28in) length each of A and B, hold them together and thread onto a yarn needle.

Work with both yarns as one strand, tie a knot 25cm (10in) along from the end without the yarn needle.

Thread the yarns through the centre of 1 disc, then bring the disc to sit next to the knot. *Leave approx. 1–2cm (⅜–¾in) gap then tie another knot and thread on the next disc; rep from * once more to add a third disc, finishing with a final knot.

Do not trim strands – leave the remaining thread.

ASSEMBLING THE BOTTOM

Using the 25cm (10in) yarn end, tie each bottom string to the wooden hoop, centred between pairs of the top strings.

Working on adjacent pairs of strings, take one strand from the left and one from the right and bring them together to meet directly beneath the suspending string. Tie together and thread all 4 strings one by one through a 3.5cm (1⅜in) pompom. Tie a knot beneath the pompom and cut one strand of A and one of B. Thread the remaining 2 yarns through the yarn needle and thread through the centre of 1 disc, then bring the disc to sit approx. 1–2cm (⅜–¾in) below the pompom. Secure with a knot as before, then add 2 more discs spaced and knotted in the same way, ending with a knot. Thread on a ball at the end and secure with a final knot. Thread the remaining ends back up through the ball and trim off. Repeat for remaining 4 bottom strings.

Sew the flowers to the frame, ensuring each flower is placed directly over the points where the top and bottom strings are tied to the hoop.

chapter 2
touch and texture

MINDFULNESS

Enjoy the sensory pleasure as the soft featherlight mohair yarn passes through your fingers. It acts as a gentle balm and can be just the thing to distract you from nagging pain or an anxious mind.

drifting thoughts corsage

Play and have fun with these flowers – there is no right or wrong, so relax and go with the flow, watching the yarn colours emerge with every stitch. Align your breath with your stitches and slow it all down. Allow thoughts to bubble up and float in and out with each petal; don't hold onto them, just let them pass without judgement. Explore this pattern using different yarns and hook sizes and see what emerges. Sew a brooch pin onto the back of your finished flower and you have the perfect gift.

SKILL RATING: ● ● ●

MATERIALS:

Hedgehog Fibres Sock Yarn (90% merino wool, 10% nylon, approx. 400m/437yds per 100g/3½oz hank) 4 ply (fingering) weight yarn

Small amount each of:
- Banana Legs
- Birthday Cake
- Villain
- Juniper
- Pinky Swear

Rico Essentials Super Kid Mohair Loves Silk (70% mohair, 30% silk, approx. 200m/218yds per 25g/⅞oz ball) 5 ply (sport) weight yarn

¼ ball each of:
- Yellow shade 017
- Fuchsia shade 021
- White shade 001
- Ice shade 002

4mm (US size G/6) crochet hook

Yarn needle

FINISHED MEASUREMENTS:

Approx. 7.5cm (3in) diameter

TENSION (GAUGE):

Exact tension is not important on this project.

ABBREVIATIONS:

See page 127.

SPECIAL ABBREVIATION:

4-dtr cl (4-double treble cluster): *[yrh] twice, insert hook in st, yrh, pull a loop through, yrh, pull through 2 loops on hook, yrh, pull through 2 loops on hook; rep from * 3 more times in same st (5 loops on hook), yrh, pull though all 5 loops to complete cluster

FOR THE FLOWER

Hold one strand of sock yarn and one of mohair yarn tog throughout.

Using any 2 colours, make a magic ring, or ch6 and join with ss in first ch to form a ring.

Round 1: Ch3 (counts as first tr), 11tr into the ring. *12 sts.*

Fasten off.

Round 2: Join 2 contrast colours in FLO of any st, *ch3, 4-dtr cl in FLO of next st, ch3, ss in FLO of next st; rep from * 5 more times. *6 petals.*

Note how the petals curl in on themselves.

Round 3: Ss in BLO (behind first petal), ch3 (counts as first tr), 1tr BLO in same st, 2tr BLO in each st to end, join with ss in 3rd of beg 3-ch. *24 sts.*

Round 4: *Ch3, 4-dtr cl in next st, ch3, ss in each of next 2 sts; rep from * 7 more times. *8 petals.*

Fasten off.

MAKING UP AND FINISHING

Sew in all yarn ends carefully.

● Move slowly through your stitches and keep your tension just so. Unravelling kid mohair is tricky so be sure to get it right first time; it's a good idea to practise the pattern with some spare DK (light worsted) yarn first.

drifting thoughts corsage **39**

MINDFULNESS

Let this pattern ground you on days when anxiety is high; allow yourself time to focus on the pleasure of making the stitches pop, whilst occupying the working memory with the simple pattern.

mad hatter's tea cosy
Combine a crazy pop of colour with a texture stitch and you have a tea cosy to brighten the gloomiest of days. Once you master the stitch you can relax into the pattern and enjoy the pleasure of seeing this cosy come to life. The delight of working the stitch can lift the spirits no end – there is something about running your fingers across the little bumps that feels both satisfying and pleasant in equal measure. This pattern is suitable for those who have mastered treble and are confident in the classic granny square.

SKILL RATING: ● ● ○

MATERIALS:
Stylecraft Special DK (100% acrylic, approx. 295m/322yds per 100g/3½oz ball) DK (light worsted) weight yarn
1 ball each of:
    Sunshine shade 1114 (A)
    Spring Green shade 1316 (B)
    Cream shade 1005 (C)
    Black shade 1002 (D)
    Lavender shade 1188 (E)
    Fiesta shade 1257 (F)

4mm (US size G/6) crochet hook
Yarn needle

FINISHED MEASUREMENTS:
22cm (8¾in) wide, 22cm (8¾in) tall

TENSION (GAUGE):
Rounds 1 and 2 = 5cm (2in) diameter, using 4mm (US size G/6) hook.

ABBREVIATIONS:
See page 127.

SPECIAL ABBREVIATION:
PC (4-tr popcorn): work 4tr all in same st, remove hook from loop and insert in top of first tr, pick up dropped loop again, yrh and join with a ss, pull tight so popcorn pops forward

FOR THE TEA COSY
SIDE 1
Using A, make a magic ring, or ch6 and join with ss in first ch to form a ring.
Round 1: Ch3 (counts as first tr throughout), 11tr into the ring. *12 sts.*
Fasten off.
Round 2: Join C in any st, ch3 (counts as first tr of PC throughout), complete PC in same st, *ch2, PC in next st; rep from * to end, join with ss in 3rd of beg 3-ch. *12 PC + twelve 2-ch sps.*
Fasten off.
Round 3: Join D in any 2-ch sp, ch3, complete PC in same sp, ch3, PC in same sp (first corner), *[ch2, PC in next st] twice, ch2, (PC, ch3, PC) in next 2-ch sp (next corner); rep from * twice, [ch2, PC in next st] twice, ch2, join with ss in first 2-ch sp of round. *16 PC + twelve 2-ch sps + four 3-ch sps.*
Fasten off.

Round 4: Join E in any 3-ch corner sp, ch3, complete PC in same sp, ch3, PC in same sp (first corner), *(ch2, PC) in each 2-ch sp to next corner, ch2, (PC, ch3, PC) in next 2-ch sp (next corner); rep from * twice, (ch2, PC) in each 2-ch sp to end, ch2, join with ss in first 2-ch sp of round. *20 PC + sixteen 2-ch sps + four 3-ch sps.* Fasten off.

Notice how the work is curving slightly to fit around the contours of your teapot.

Round 5: Using F, rep round 4. *24 PC + twenty 2-ch sps + four 3-ch sps.*

Round 6: Using B, rep round 4. *28 PC + twenty-four 2-ch sps + four 3-ch sps.*

Round 7: Using C and D, rep round 4 alt colours to work one PC in C and next in D, carrying yarn not in use and changing colour on first ch after each PC. *32 PC + thirty-two 2-ch sps + four 3-ch sps.*

Round 8: Join A in any sp, ch3, 3tr in same st, complete PC in same sp, (ch2, PC) in each 2-ch or 3-ch sp around (no corners on this round), ending with ch2, join with ss in first 2-ch sp of round. Fasten off. *32 PC + thirty-two 2-ch sps.*

Round 9: Join F in any sp, ch1 (does not count as st), 2dc in each 2-ch sp around, join with ss in first st. *64 sts.*

With RS facing, using F, work surface crochet (see page 126) around outer edge of round 1.

Fasten off.

SIDE 2

Using B, make a magic ring, or ch6 and join with ss in first ch to form a ring.

Round 1: Using B, rep round 1 of side 1.
Round 2: Using D, rep round 2 of side 1.
Round 3: Using C, rep round 3 of side 1.
Round 4: Using A, rep round 4 of side 1.
Round 5: Rep round 5 of side 1.
Round 6: Using E, rep round 4 of side 1.
Round 7: Rep round 7 of side 1.
Round 8: Using B, rep round 8 of side 1.
Round 9: Rep round 9 of side 1.

With RS facing, using F, work surface crochet around outer edge of round 1.

Fasten off.

MAKING UP AND FINISHING

Place both sides around the teapot with RS facing outward. Line up the 'corners' and, using F, sew them from the base to the bottom of the spout (approx. three popcorns). Leaving a space large enough to fit comfortably over the spout, sew all the way round to the top of the handle. Fasten off.

Sew in all yarn ends carefully.

Make a pompom (see page 125) in F and sew onto the top.

● To make the cosy for a smaller teapot, omit rounds 5 and 6.

peaceful cushion cover

This project is close to my heart as it's the exact same yarns and pattern I worked whilst recovering from breast cancer. The hook and yarn are easy to hold and the pattern (once mastered) flows gently and requires nothing more than a little peace and quiet as you count the stitches in each round. One circle was all I could manage in a sitting, but seeing the colours fall from the hook gave me the boost I needed whilst having treatment. I've chosen pure merino wool for the border colours to compliment the pure wool Noro, because sometimes a little luxury is what we need to feed the spirit and soul.

MINDFULNESS

Switch off from all decision making and let this glorious yarn do all the talking. Sit back and relax as you create circles of colour following this simple rhythmical pattern. After making the circles, discover the delight of seeing how the colours are transformed by either the black or white yarn.

SKILL RATING: ● ● ○

MATERIALS:

Noro Kureyon (100% wool, approx. 100m/109yds per 50g/1¾oz ball) Aran (worsted) weight yarn
  1 ball each of:
    Shade 369 (A)
    Shade 319 (B)

Rico Essentials Soft Merino Aran (100% wool, approx. 100m/109yds per 50g/1¾oz ball) Aran (worsted) weight yarn
  1 ball each of:
    Black shade 090 (C)
    Natural shade 060 (D)

4.5mm (US size 7) crochet hook

Yarn needle

35cm (14in) square cushion pad

FINISHED MEASUREMENTS:

Each square (once blocked): 12cm (4¾in) square
Cushion cover: 36cm (14¼in) square

TENSION (GAUGE):

Rounds 1–4 = 6cm (2¼in) diameter, using 4.5mm (US size 7) hook.

ABBREVIATIONS:

See page 127

FOR THE COVER

CIRCLES (make 9 in each of A and B)

Using A or B, make a magic ring, or ch6 and join with ss in first ch to form a ring.

Round 1: Ch1 (does not count as st throughout), 6dc into the ring, join with ss in first dc. *6 sts.*

Round 2: Ch1, 2dc in each st to end, join with ss in first dc. *12 sts.*

Round 3: Ch1, [2dc in next st, 1dc in next st] 6 times, join with ss in in first dc. *18 sts.*

Round 4: Ch1, [2dc in next st, 1dc in each of next 2 sts] 6 times, join with ss in first dc. *24 sts.*

Round 5: Ch1, [2dc in next st, 1dc in each of next 3 sts] 6 times, join with ss in first dc. *30 sts.*

Round 6: Ch1, [2dc in next st, 1dc in each of next 4 sts] 6 times, join with ss in first dc. *36 sts.*

Fasten off.

SQUARING THE CIRCLES (make 9 in each of C and D)

Taking any circle, join C or D in any st.

Round 1: Ch3 (counts as first tr), 1tr in same st, *1tr in next st, 1htr in each of next 2 sts, 1dc in each of next 2 sts, 1htr in each of next 2 sts, 1tr in next st, (2tr, ch2, 2tr) in next st (corner); rep from * twice more, 1tr in next st, 1htr in each of next 2 sts, 1dc in each of next 2 sts, 1htr in each of next 2 sts, 1tr in next st, (2tr, ch2) in beg st, join with ss in 3rd of beg 3-ch. *48 tr + four 2-ch sps.*

Round 2: Ch1 (does not count as st), 2dc in corner 2-ch sp, *miss next st, 1dc in each of next 11 sts, (2dc, ch2, 2dc) in corner 2-ch sp; rep from * twice, miss next st, 1dc in each of next 11 sts, (2dc, ch2) in beg corner st, join with ss in first dc. *60 dc + four 2-ch sps.*

Fasten off.

MAKING UP AND FINISHING

Block all the squares before joining.

Lay nine of the squares out in three rows of three in any sequence you like. Using a yarn needle and matching background yarn and with squares RS facing, join together using whip stitch (see page 125), working into the outside loop only of the corresponding edge stitches. Do not pull the yarn too tightly when sewing. Make a second large square with the other nine squares.

BORDER

Join a matching yarn (C or D) in any corner sp of large square, ch1 (counts as 1dc), 1dc in same sp, *1dc in each st (but do not work dc in stitched joins) to corner sp, (2dc, ch2, 2dc) in corner sp; rep from * to beg corner, (2dc, ch2) in beg 2-ch sp, join with ss in beg 1-ch.

Fasten off, then rep on the second square.

JOINING THE PIECES

Position the two large squares with WS together and matching the stitches across each side edge – as you join the squares, when three sides of the large square have been joined insert the cushion pad before joining the final side. Working through both squares, join A or B in any 2-ch sp corner, and ch1 (counts as first dc). Work a double crochet seam (see page 124) to join the two pieces, working (1dc, ch2, 1dc) in each corner sp, ending (1dc, ch2) in the beg corner, join with a ss in beg 1-ch.

Fasten off and sew in all yarn ends carefully.

● A word of caution – the yarn quantities listed are exact to the very last thread: one ball of the Noro colours will make 9 circles with just enough yarn left over to work the border. The same goes for the Rico yarn, so if you are nervous of running out you may want to buy an extra ball of each.

openwork winter

scarf This scarf is all about keeping the
tension super loose, so that you create a lovely,
light, airy drape to the finished piece. If your tension
is usually tight then you may want to practise a few
rows to get a feel for working loosely – or go up a hook size.

SKILL RATING: ● ● ●

MATERIALS:

Rico Creative Light Melange Glitz
(44% wool, 44% acrylic, 10%
polyamide, 2% polyester, approx.
150m/164yds per 50g/1¾oz ball)
chunky (bulky) weight yarn
  1 ball each of:
    Ecru Mix shade 001 (A
    Grey Mix shade 002 (B)

Rico Fashion Light Luxury (74% alpaca,
22% wool, 4% polyamide, approx.
130m/142yds per 50g/1¾oz ball) super
chunky (super bulky) weight yarn
    1 ball of Neon Red shade 021 (C)

9mm (US size M/13) hook

FINISHED MEASUREMENTS:

31cm (12¼in) wide, 180cm (71in) long
(excluding tassels)

TENSION (GAUGE):

8 sts x 4.5 rows = 10cm (4in) over
treble, using 9mm (US size M/13) hook.

ABBREVIATIONS:

See page 127.

FOR THE SCARF

Using A, ch26.
Row 1: 1tr in 4th ch from hook (missed 3-ch counts as tr), 1tr in each ch to
end. *24 sts.*
Row 2: Ch3 (counts as first tr throughout), 1tr in each of next 22 sts, 1tr in
3rd of beg 3-ch from prev row. *24 tr.*
Rows 3–13: Rep row 2, changing to C on last tr of row 13.
Rows 14 and 15: Using C, rep row 2, changing to B on last tr of row 15.
Rows 16 and 17: Using B, rep row 2, changing to C on last tr of row 17,
carrying yarn up edge and keeping it very loose. Avoid pulling tightly as this
will distort shape of scarf.
Rows 18 and 19: Using C, rep row 2, changing to B on last tr of row 19.
Rows 20 and 21: Using B, rep row 2, changing to C on last tr of row 21.
Rep rows 18–21 a further 12 times until you have made 14 stripes in C and
14 in B in total, changing to yarn A on last tr of last row.
Fasten off C and B.
Rows 70–82: Using A, rep row 2.
Fasten off.

- Make the foundation chain very loose by either keeping your tension (gauge) loose, or use a 10mm (US size N/15) hook if you have one in your collection. Remember to change back to a 9mm (US size M/13) hook after the chain is completed.

- Work into stitches and not between the posts, which can sometimes happen when starting out in crochet.

- It is very easy to miss the last treble made into the top of the turning chain from the previous row, so count your stitches on every row until you are completely confident.

- When changing colour, introduce the new colour on the last yarn round hook of the current row.

- Keep both colours attached to the work throughout, bringing the yarn up to the current row when required. Keep the yarn very loose – avoid pulling it tight as this will distort the shape of the scarf. This means that along one side of your scarf you will see the grey and the pink yarns being carried up to the next colour change.

MAKING UP AND FINISHING

Sew in all yarn ends carefully.

ADD THE TASSELS

Cut 24 lengths of each colour, each 20cm (8in) long. Holding one strand of each colour together, make a tassel (see page 125). Attach one tassel to first and last stitches of the foundation row, and space another ten tassels equally between them. Repeat for the other end of the scarf. Trim the tassels to the desired length.

openwork winter scarf **47**

mindfulness cowl

This cowl, with its simple repeat pattern and working a new yarn with every row, is designed to give you a mini mindful break. Aim to complete three rows in a sitting and be aware of the different texture of the yarns.

SKILL RATING: ● ○ ○

MATERIALS:

Adriafil Zebrino (53% wool, 47% acrylic, approx. 125m/136yds per 50g/1¾oz ball) Aran (worsted) weight yarn
  1 ball each of:
    Shade 66 (A)
    Shade 62 (B)

Rico Essentials Super Kid Mohair Loves Silk (70% mohair, 30% silk, approx. 200m/219yds per 25g/⅞oz ball) 4 ply (sport) weight yarn
  1 x ball of Silver shade 008 (C)

4.5mm (US size 7) crochet hook

Yarn needle

FINISHED MEASUREMENTS:

79cm (31½in) long x 28cm (11in) wide (flat and blocked before joining ends)

TENSION (GAUGE):

12 sts x 13 rows = 10cm (4in) over double crochet, using 4.5mm (US size 7) hook.

ABBREVIATIONS:

See page 127.

FOR THE COWL

Using A, ch36.

Row 1: 1dc in 3rd ch from hook, 1dc in each ch to end, changing to B on last st, turn. *34 sts.*

Row 2: Using B, ch1 (does not count as st throughout), 1dc in each st to end, changing to C on last st, turn.

Row 3: Using C, ch2 (counts as first htr throughout), 1htr FLO in each st to end, changing to A on last st, turn.

Row 4: Using A, ch1, 1dc in each st to end, changing to B on last st, turn.

Row 5: Using B, ch1, 1dc in each st to end, changing to C on last st, turn.

Row 6: Using C, ch2, 1htr FLO in each st to end, changing to A on last st, turn.

Rows 7–90: Rep patt rows 4–6, changing yarn on each row in sequence A, B, C, ending with a C row.

Fasten off.

MAKING UP AND FINISHING

Sew in all yarn ends carefully and block.

With the scarf laid out flat, take the corners of one end and flip them over to create a twist in the middle of the scarf. Using A, join the two ends together with whip stitch (see page 125, preserving the twist.

● Join in the new colour on the final yarn round hook of the current round. Do not fasten off the old colour because you will be picking the yarn up again every third row.

meditation rug

A super-soft rug that feels like you are sitting on a cloud and is perfect for meditation! This is a fantastically quick project to make – the yarn has super squish appeal and once you get the hang of working with such a large hook (or your fingers), it becomes something of a mission to get it made in one sitting. I found the trickiest part was working the first two rounds, because it takes a little getting used to.

SKILL RATING: ● ● ○

MATERIALS:

Rico Creative Pom (100% polyester, approx. 20m/21yds per 200g/7oz ball) super chunky (super bulky) weight yarn
  3 balls of Grey shade 005 (A)
  1 ball of White shade 001 (B)

20mm (US size S) crochet hook (or use fingers)

FINISHED MEASUREMENTS:

83cm (33in) diameter

TENSION (GAUGE):

Round 1 = 15cm (6in) diameter, using 20mm (US size S) hook.

ABBREVIATIONS:

See page 127.

FOR THE RUG

Using A and either a 20mm (US size S) hook or your thumb and fingers, ch2.
Round 1: 6dc in first ch, join with ss in first dc. *6 sts.*
Round 2: Ch1 (does not count as st), 2dc in each st to end, join with ss in first dc. *12 sts.*
Round 3: Ch2 (counts as 1dc + ch1 throughout), [(1dc, ch1) into next st] 11 times, using B, join with ss in first of beg 2-ch. Do not cut A. *12 sts + twelve 1-ch sps.*
Round 4: Using B, ch3 (counts as 1dc + ch2), [1dc in next 1-ch sp, ch2] 11 times, using A, join with ss in first of beg 3-ch. *12 sts + twelve 2-ch sps.*
Round 5: Ch2, [2dc in next 2-ch sp, ch1] 11 times, 1dc in last 1-ch sp, join with ss in first of beg 2-ch. *24 sts + twelve 1-ch sps.*
Round 6: Ss in first 1-ch sp, ch4 (counts as 1dc + ch3), [1dc in next 1-ch sp, ch3] 11 times, join with ss in first of beg 4-ch. *12 sts + twelve 3-ch sps.*
Fasten off A, leaving 25cm (10in) end.
Round 7: Join B in any 3-ch sp, ch2 (counts as 1dc + ch1 throughout), 1dc in same sp, ch2, [(1dc, ch1, 1dc) in next 3-ch sp, ch2] 11 times, join with ss in first of beg 2-ch. *24 sts + twelve 1-ch sps + twelve 2-ch sps.*
Fasten off B, leaving 25cm (10in) end.
Round 8: Join A in any 1-ch sp from prev round, ch2, [(1dc, ch1, 1dc) in next 2-ch sp, ch1, 1dc in next 1-ch sp, ch1] 11 times, (1dc, ch1, 1dc) in next 2-ch sp, ch1, join with ss in first of beg 2-ch. *36 sts + thirty-six 1-ch sps.*

Round 9: Ss in first 1-ch sp, ch2, [1dc in next 1-ch sp, ch2, 1dc in next 1-ch sp, ch1] 11 times, 1dc in next 1-ch sp, ch2, join with ss in first of beg 2-ch.
Fasten off.

MAKING UP AND FINISHING

Weave in all yarn ends carefully.

● The easiest way to fasten in all the yarn ends is simply to use your fingers and weave them in and around the stitches.

● When joining in a new colour or new ball in the middle of your work, remember to leave 20cm (8in) ends at the end of the current ball and the beginning of the new ball so you'll have enough to weave in all the ends.

● Don't pull the yarn too tight (almost impossible to do this but still it's worth saying) – and if you do need to pull any stitches out, take it slow and ease them with your fingers as the yarn likes to cling to itself.

ripple wrap of mindful imperfections

The wonderful chevron effect in this wrap is created by working extra stitches in one place for a peak and missing stitches for a valley. Hidden within it are little imperfections, mistakes I have made whilst working the pattern, which I've used to practise acceptance and letting go. To observe and not change; to notice and to be OK with what I find. Crochet is a journey and sometimes the 'mistakes' we make can be worked into our creation – not everything needs to be pulled out and made perfect.

SKILL RATING: ● ● ●

MATERIALS:

Scheepjes Our Tribe (70% wool, 30% polyamide, approx. 420m/459yds per 100g/3½oz ball) 4 ply (fingering) weight yarn
1 ball each of:
Lavender Smoke shade 883 (A)
Miss Neriss shade 966 (B)
Look At What I Made shade 972 (C)

Scheepjes Mohair Rhythm (70% mohair, 30% microfibre, approx. 200m/218yds per 25g/⅞oz ball) lace weight yarn
2 balls of Merengue shade 686 (D)

4.5mm (US size 7) crochet hook
Yarn needle

FINISHED MEASUREMENTS:

Approx. 43cm (17in) wide x 200cm (80in) long

TENSION (GAUGE):

(10htr, 2htr, ch2, 2htr) in same st to form peak + 10 htr = 10cm (4in), 9 rows = 10cm (4in), using 4.5mm (US size 7) hook.

ABBREVIATIONS:

See page 127.

SPECIAL ABBREVIATION:

crossed2tr (crossed 2 treble): miss next st, 1tr in next st then work 1tr in missed st (working over first tr)

● Work in the back loop only on all rows except when working with yarn D.

● You'll begin each row with 'ch2, 1htr in each of next 2 sts, miss next st' and work the last 4 sts on all rows 'miss 2 sts, 1htr in each of last 2 sts'.

● To make a peak work: (2htr, ch2, 2htr) and to make a valley 'miss 3 sts'.

● The pattern is in multiples of 24 + 4 stitches.

FOR THE WRAP

Using A, ch102.

Row 1: 1htr in 3rd ch from hook (missed 2-ch does not count as st), 1htr in next ch, miss next ch, *1htr in each of next 10 ch, (2htr, ch3, 2htr) in next ch (for peak), 1htr in each of next 10 ch, miss next 3 ch (for valley); rep from * 3 more times, ending final rep with miss next 2 ch (for 5th and final valley), 1htr in each of last 2 ch.

Row 2: Ch2 (does not count as st throughout), 1htr BLO in each of first 2 sts, miss next st, *1htr BLO in each of next 10 sts, (2htr, ch3, 2htr) in next ch sp (for peak), 1htr BLO in each of next 10 sts, miss next 3 sts (for valley); rep from * 3 more times, ending final rep with miss next 2 sts (for last valley), 1htr BLO in each of last 2 sts.

Rows 3–10: Rep row 2.

Rows 11–14: Using B, rep row 2.

Rows 15 and 16 (non-BLO rows): Using D, work as row 2 but work every htr through both loops.

Rows 17–20: Using B, rep row 2 (working in BLO again).

Row 21 (crossed tr row): Using A and working in BLO throughout, ch2, 1tr in each of next 2 sts, miss next st, *[work crossed2tr over next 2 sts] 5 times, (2tr, ch2, 2tr) in next ch sp (first peak), [work crossed2tr over next 2 sts] 5 times, miss next 3 sts (for valley); rep from * 3 more times, ending final rep with miss next 2 sts (for last valley), 1tr in each of last 2 sts.

Rows 11–21 form patt, rep them 3 more times.

Cont to rep patt rows 11–21, changing colour as foll:

Row 55: C.

Row 56–58: B.

Rows 59 and 60: D

Row 61: C.

Rows 62 and 63: B.

Row 64: C.

Row 65 (crossed tr row): A.

Row 66: B.

Row 67: C.

Row 68: B.

Row 69: C.

Rows 70 and 71 (non-BLO rows): D.

Rows 72 and 73: C.

Row 74: B.

Row 75: C.

Row 76 (crossed tr row): A.

Rows 77–80: C.

Rows 81–82 (non-BLO rows): D.

Rows 83–86: C.

Row 87 (crossed tr row): A.

Rows 88–109: Rep rows 77–87 twice more.

Rows 110–113: C.

Rows 114–115 (non-BLO rows): D.

Rows 116–119: C.

Rows 120–129: Using A, rep row 2.

Fasten off.

MAKING UP AND FINISHING

Sew in all yarn ends carefully.

comfort mittens

These little mitts are so simple to make – the squares are joined to make a tube with a hole for the thumb! Each square has a squidgy puff stitch centre, for extra insulation on a cold day.

MATERIALS:

Lang Yarns Mille Colori Baby (100% wool, approx. 190m/207yds per 50g/1¾oz ball) 4 ply (fingering) weight yarn
  1 ball of shade 061 (A)

Scheepjes Alpaca Rhythm (80% alpaca, 20% wool, approx. 200m/218yds per 25g/⅞oz ball) lace weight yarn
  1 ball of Paso shade 662 (B)

Scheepjes Mohair Rhythm (70% mohair, 30% microfibre, approx. 200m/218yds per 25g/⅞oz ball) lace weight yarn
  1 ball of Merengue shade 686 (C)
  1 ball of Vogue shade 681 (D)

4mm (US size G/6) crochet hook

Yarn needle

FINISHED MEASUREMENTS:

20cm (8in) circumference x 17cm (6¾in) long

TENSION (GAUGE):

Rounds 1–3 = 5.5cm (2¼in) square, using 4mm (US size G/6) hook.

ABBREVIATIONS:

See page 127.

SPECIAL ABBREVIATION:

PS (puff stitch): *yrh, insert hook into st and pull a loop through keeping the yarn loops long; rep from * 4 more times into same st, yrh and draw through all loops on hook, 1ch to close st

FOR THE MITTENS

PUFF CENTRES (make 24 – 12 per mitten)

Using a strand of A and C held tog, make a magic ring, or ch6 and join with ss in first ch to form a ring.

Round 1: Ch1 (does not count as a st), 8dc in ring. *8 sts.*

Round 2: Ch3 (does not count as a st), 1PS in first dc, ch2 (makes 3-ch sp), *1PS in next dc, ch2; rep from * to end, join with ss in top of beg PS. *8 PS + eight 3-ch sps.* Fasten off A.

Finish and join squares using join-as-you-go method (see page 122) to make a rectangle of 3 rows of 4 squares, as foll:

STARTER SQUARE

Round 3: Join B and C tog in any 3-ch sp, hold as one strand throughout. Ch2 (counts as first htr throughout), 2htr in same 3-ch sp (makes half corner), 3dc in next 3-ch sp, *(3htr, ch2, 3htr) in next ch-3 sp, 3dc in next 3-ch sp; rep from * twice more, 3htr in beg 3-ch sp, ch2, join with ss in 2nd of beg 2-ch.
Fasten off B and C.

SECOND SQUARE

Round 3: Join B and C tog in any 3-ch sp, hold as one strand throughout. Ch2, 2htr in same 3-ch sp (makes half corner), 3dc in next 3-ch sp, 3htr in next 3-ch sp then instead of ch2 for corner sp, insert hook in corner sp of starter square from underneath, 1dc in corner of starter square (counts as first of 2-ch for corner sp), ch1, work second 3-htr group in corner sp of second square as usual. Cont joining squares tog, making 1dc in next side sp between 3-htr and 3-dc of starter square followed by 3dc in next 3-ch sp of second square, 1dc in next sp between 3-dc and 3-htr of starter square, 3htr in next 3-ch sp in second square, 1dc in next corner sp of starter square, ch1, 3htr group in same corner 3-ch sp of second square. When second square is joined to starter square along one side, cont around to finish round 3 as normal.

Cont to join squares in this way throughout. When joining a square to two prev squares at a shared corner, replace both corner ch with 1dc in each adjoining square.

Rep to make a rectangle of 3 rows of 4 squares for second mitten.

MAKING UP AND FINISHING

Sew in all yarn ends carefully.

Lay each mitten flat and then fold in half with RS together, joining the two short ends. Using a length of B and C held tog, sew the ends of row 1 and row 3 together using whip stitch (see page 125), and leaving row 2 open for the thumbhole.

THUMBHOLE EDGING

Turn each mitten RS out. Join B and C in any st around thumbhole.

Round 1: Ch1 (counts as dc throughout), 1dc in each of next 19 sts around thumbhole, join with ss in beg 1-ch. *20 sts.*

Round 2: Ch1, 1dc in each st to end, join with ss in beg 1-ch.
Fasten off and sew in ends.

chapter 3
mindful meditation

MINDFULNESS

This project requires careful counting on the first 7 to 9 rounds, so make this part of the mindful practice. Slow your stitches and get a gentle rhythm going between your breath and the flow of the hook with the yarn. There's no rush and the slower you go the easier it becomes.

boho baskets

Play with the colours on these sweet little baskets and go where your heart takes you. I've worked some of them in graded tones from light to dark, but the multi-coloured one is a glorious melange of lots of different colours. Each basket becomes its own unique creation just like you.

SKILL RATING: ● ● ●

MATERIALS:

Scheepjes Cahlista (100% cotton, approx. 85m/92yds per 50g/1¾oz ball) Aran (worsted) weight yarn

Blue basket:
1 ball each of:
Bridal White shade 105
Bluebell shade 173
Cyan shade 397
Electric Blue shade 201

Pink basket:
1 ball each of:
Bridal White shade 105
Powder Pink shade 238
Fresia shade 519
Shocking Pink shade 114

Green basket:
1 ball each of:
Bridal White shade 105
Primrose shade 522
Lime Juice shade 392
Apple Granny shade 513

Large mutli-coloured basket:
⅓ ball each of all of above plus:
Royal Orange shade 189
Tangerine shade 281
Yellow Gold shade 208
Light Orchid shade 226

4.5mm (US size 7) crochet hook

Stitch marker

Yarn needle

FINISHED MEASUREMENTS:

Blue basket: 8cm (3¼in) diameter, 7cm (2¾in) deep

Green basket: 9cm (3½in) diameter, 7cm (2¾in) deep

Pink basket: 10cm (4in) diameter, 9.5cm (3¾in) deep

Multi-coloured basket: 14cm (5½in) diameter, 10cm (4in) deep

TENSION (GAUGE):

10 sts x 13 rows = 10cm (4in) over double crochet, using 4.5mm (US size 7) hook and two strands of yarn held together.

ABBREVIATIONS:

See page 127.

FOR THE BASKETS

BLUE BASKET

Hold two strands of different colours tog throughout.
Using first 2 colours held tog, make a magic ring, or ch6 and join with ss in first ch to form a ring.
Round 1: Ch1 (does not count as st throughout), 6dc into the ring, join with ss in first dc. *6 sts.*
Round 2: Ch1, 2dc in each st to end, join with ss in first dc. *12 sts.*
Round 3: Ch1, [1dc in next st, 2dc in next st] 6 times, join with ss in first dc. *18 sts.*
Round 4: Ch1, [1dc in each of next 2 sts, 2dc in next st] 6 times, join with ss in first dc. *24 sts.*
Round 5: Ch1, [1dc in each of next 3 sts, 2dc in next st] 6 times, join with ss in first dc. *30 sts.*

MAKE THE SIDES

Beg to work in cont spiral with 1dc in each st, changing colour as desired. PM in first st and move up as each round is completed.
As sides begin to 'curl' up, turn work inside out, cont to crochet in anti-clockwise direction.
When you have reached desired height, join last round with ss in first st.
Fasten off.

● Keep your tension (gauge) tight as this helps with the stability of the basket. Working a tight tension (gauge) with two strands held as one can make your hand and arm ache, so a little rest every few rows really helps.

● The base for the baskets is worked in rounds joined with a ss. Each round begins with ch1, which is not counted as a stitch. To avoid losing a stitch, always work the first dc into the same stitch at the base of the beginning ch1.

● To blend the colours gently, cut one of the yarns leaving a 10cm (4in) end and introduce a new colour on the next yarn round hook, working over all the yarn ends as you go. For dramatic colour changes as on the multi-coloured basket, cut both yarns leaving 10cm (4in) ends and work one more double crochet in these two colours, changing to two new colours on the last yarn round hook and working over all yarn ends.

GREEN BASKET

Work as blue basket to end of round 5.
Round 6: Ch1, [1dc in each of next 4 sts, 2dc in next st] 6 times, join with ss in first dc. *36 sts.*
Work sides as Blue Basket.

PINK BASKET

Work as green basket to end of round 6.
Round 7: Ch1, [1dc in each of next 5 sts, 2dc in next st] 6 times, join with ss in first dc. *42 sts.*
Work sides as Blue Basket.

MULTI-COLOURED BASKET

Work as pink basket to end of round 7.
Round 8: Ch1, [1dc in each of next 6 sts, 2dc in next st] 6 times, join with ss in first dc. *48 sts.*
Round 9: Ch1, [1dc in each of next 7 sts, 2dc in next st] 6 times, join with ss in first dc. *54 sts.*
Work sides as Blue Basket.

MAKING UP AND FINISHING

Sew in all yarn ends carefully.

mandala in a hoop

Take your time on each round of this mandala and enjoy the fresh spring colours of the yarn. It is important to count the stitches as you go, and the simple act of counting acts as a mantra that really can slow your thoughts right down.

MATERIALS:

Rico Ricorumi DK (100% cotton, approx. 58m/63yds per 25g/⅞oz ball) DK (light worsted) weight yarn
  1 ball each of:
    Cream shade 002 (A)
    Light Green shade 046 (B)
    Fuchsia shade 014 (C)
    Lilac shade 017 (D)

4mm (US size G/6) crochet hook

Yarn needle

30cm (12in) diameter embroidery hoop inner

FINISHED MEASUREMENTS:

29cm (11½in) diameter

TENSION (GAUGE):

Rounds 1 to 4 = 8cm (3¼in) diameter, using 4mm (US size G/6) hook.

ABBREVIATIONS:

See page 127.

SPECIAL ABBREVIATIONS:

4-htr cl (4-half treble cluster): yrh, insert hook in st, yrh, pull a loop through (3 loops on hook), yrh, pull through 2 loops on hook (2 loops on hook), yrh, insert hook in next st, yrh, pull a loop through (4 loops on hook), yrh, pull through 2 loops on hook (3 loops on hook), yrh, insert hook in next st, yrh, pull a loop through (5 loops on hook), yrh, pull through 2 loops on hook (4 loops on hook), yrh, pull through all 4 loops to gather cluster tog

FPhtr (front post half treble): yrh, take hook from front around post of st in prev round, yrh, pull a loop through (3 loops on hook), yrh, pull through all 3 loops

FPhtr dec (front post half treble decrease): yrh, insert hook from front around post of st in prev round, yrh, pull a loop through (3 loops on hook), yrh, pull through 2 loops (2 loops on hook), yrh, take hook from front around post of next st in prev round, yrh, pull a loop though (4 loops on hook), yrh, pull through all 4 loops

MP (make picot): ch3, ss in 3rd ch from hook

PC (3-tr popcorn): work 3tr all in same st, remove hook from loop and insert from front to back in top of first tr made, pick up dropped loop and pull through, ch1

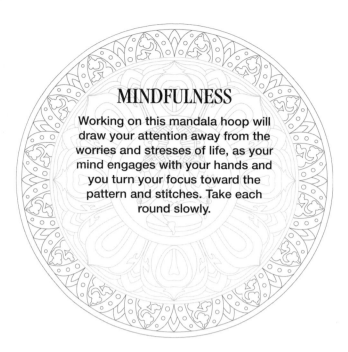

MINDFULNESS

Working on this mandala hoop will draw your attention away from the worries and stresses of life, as your mind engages with your hands and you turn your focus toward the pattern and stitches. Take each round slowly.

FOR THE MANDALA

Using A, make a magic ring, or ch6 and join with ss in first ch to form a ring.

Round 1: Ch1 (does not count as st), 8dc into the ring, join with ss in first dc. *8 sts.*
Fasten off.

Round 2: Join B in any st, ch3 (counts as first tr throughout), 2tr in same st, ch3, PC in next st, ch3, (PC, 3ch) in each st to end, join with ss in top of beg 3-ch. *8 PC + eight 3-ch sps.*

Round 3: Join C in any 3-ch sp, ch3, (2tr, ch2, PC) in same sp, ch2, *(PC, ch2, PC) in next 3-ch sp, ch2; rep from * to end, join with ss in 3rd of beg 3-ch. *16 PC + sixteen 2-ch sps.*
Fasten off.

Round 4: Join D in any 2-ch sp, ch1 (counts as first dc throughout), 2dc in same sp, 3dc in each 2-ch sp to end, join with ss in beg 1-ch. *48 sts.*
Fasten off.

Round 5: Join B in first dc of any 3-dc group in prev row, ch1, [ch3, miss 2 sts, 1dc] 15 times, ch3, miss last 2 sts, join with ss in beg 1-ch. *16 dc + sixteen 3-ch sps.*
Fasten off.

Round 6: Join A in any 3-ch sp, ch2 (counts as first htr throughout), 3htr in same sp, *4htr in next 3-ch sp; rep from * to end, join with ss into 2nd of beg 2-ch. *64 sts.*
Fasten off.

Round 7: Join C in first htr of any 4-htr group in prev round, ch4 (counts as 1dtr), miss 3 sts, *(1dtr, ch4, 1dtr) in next st, miss 3 sts; rep from * 14 times, 1dtr in same sp as beg 4-ch, ch4, join with ss in 4th of beg 4-ch. *32 dtr + sixteen 4-ch sps.*
Fasten off.

Round 8: Join D in any 4-ch sp, ch2, 5htr in same sp, FPhtr dec over next 2 dtr, [6htr in next 4-ch sp, FPhtr dec over next 2 dtr] 15 times, join with ss in 2nd of beg 2-ch. *96 htr + 16 FPhtr dec.*
Fasten off.

Round 9: Join A around front post of any FPhtr dec from prev round, ch5 (counts as 1FPhtr and ch3), *miss 3 sts, 1dc in next st, ch3, miss 2 sts, 1FPhtr in next FPhtr dec from prev round; rep from * to end, finishing last rep with ch3, miss last 2 sts, join with ss in 2nd of beg 5-ch, do not fasten off. *16 FPhtr +16 dc + 32 3-ch sps.*

Round 10: Ch1, 3dc in first 3-ch sp, 4dc in each 3-ch sp around, join with ss in beg 1-ch. *128 sts.*
Fasten off.

Round 11: Join B in any st, ch2, 1htr in each st to end, join with ss in 2nd of beg 2-ch.
Fasten off.

Round 12: Join C in any st above dc from round 9, ch2 (counts as first st of 4-htr cl), complete 4-htr cl over next 3 sts, [4-htr cl, ch5] to end. *Thirty-two 4-htr cl + thirty-two 5-ch sps.*
Fasten off.

Round 13: Join A in any 5-ch sp, ch2, (4tr, 1htr) in same sp, *(1htr, 4tr, 1htr) in next 5-ch sp; rep from * to end, join with ss in 2nd of 2-ch. *192 sts.*

Round 14: Join D around front post of any 4-htr cl from round 12, ch2 (counts as 1FPhtr), *ch3, miss 3 sts, (ss, MP, ss) in next st, ch3, miss 2 sts, 1FPhtr in next 4-htr cl from round 12; rep from * to end, finishing last rep with ch3, miss last 2 sts, ss in 2nd of beg 5-ch.
Fasten off.

MAKING UP AND FINISHING

Sew in all yarn ends carefully.

Using D, join the mandala to the hoop, sewing through the picot from back to front and then taking the yarn up and over the hoop.

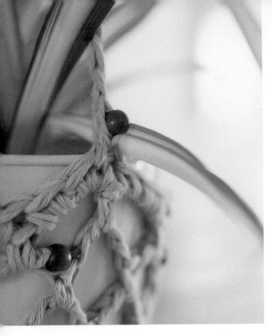

hanging gardens plant holder

These little hanging baskets can be adapted to fit any size pot, so you can start small and crochet up a bigger hanger as your plant grows. I've worked a version of this pattern to include beads, which are a great way of adding a pop of colour to your crochet. If you have never worked beads into your crochet then now is the time to embrace the experience of learning something new!

SKILL RATING: ● ● ○

MATERIALS:

Rico Creative Cotton Aran (100% cotton, approx. 85m/92yds per 50g/1¾oz ball) Aran (worsted) weight yarn
  1 ball each of:
    Orange shade 74 (A)
    Fuchsia shade 13 (B)
    Sky Blue shade 37 (C)
    Light Green shade 40 (D)

6mm (US size J/10) crochet hook

Stitch marker

Yarn needle

48 beads (optional, medium pot only)

FINISHED MEASUREMENTS:

Small pot: to fit 6.5cm (2½in) base pot
Medium pot: to fit 10cm (4in) base pot

TENSION (GAUGE):

Rounds 1–2 = 7.5cm (3in) diameter, using 6mm (US size J/10) hook.

ABBREVIATIONS:

See page 127.

SPECIAL ABBREVIATIONS:

place bead dc: insert hook in st, yrh, pull a loop through, bring bead up to hook, yrh, pull through both loops on hook

place bead ch: bring bead up to hook and ch1

FOR THE HOLDER

SMALL POT

Working with A and B held tog throughout, make a magic ring, or ch6 and join with ss in first ch to form a ring.
Round 1: Ch3 (counts as first tr throughout), 11tr into the ring, join with ss in 3rd of beg 3-ch. *12 sts.*
Round 2: Ch3, 1tr in same st, 2tr in each st to end, join with ss in 3rd of beg 3-ch. *24 sts.*
Round 3: Ch1 (counts as first dc), ch1, [miss next st, 1dc in foll st, ch1] 11 times, miss last st, join with ss in beg 1-ch. *12 dc + twelve 1-ch sps.*
You will see the sides beg to curl up slightly.
Round 4: [1dc in next 1-ch sp, ch4] 12 times, join last 4-ch with ss in first 4-ch. Beg to work in cont spiral. PM in first st and move up as each round is completed.
Round 5: [Ch4, 1dc in next 4-ch sp] to end.
Rep round 5 until desired height is reached.
Final round: [2dc in each 4-ch sp] to end, join with ss in first dc. *24 dc.*
Fasten off.

SMALL POT HANGING STRANDS

At this point the pot cover is looking very floppy and shapeless but fear not! Work with two strands held tog throughout.
Strand 1: Join yarn in sp between any 2-dc group, ch60 (more for longer hanging depth).
Fasten off, leaving 70cm (28in) end.
Strands 2, 3 and 4: Count 6 sts from prev strand, join yarn in next sp between dc, ch60.
Fasten off, leaving 20cm (8in) end.

MEDIUM POT

Thread all beads onto either C or D, then cont working with C and D held tog throughout.
Work base as small pot to end of round 2.

● As you work the beads will rise up to the hook and you will need to keep pushing them down until you wish to use one.

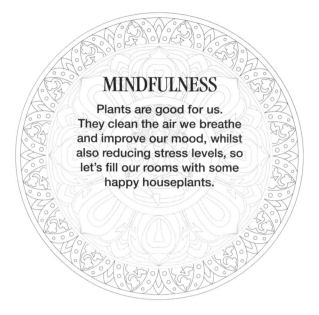

Round 3: Ch3, 1tr in same st, [1tr in next st, 2tr in next st] 11 times, 1tr in next st, join with ss in 3rd of beg 3-ch. *36 sts.*

Round 4: Ch1 (counts as first dc), ch2, [miss next 2 sts, 1dc in foll st, ch2] 11 times, miss last 2 sts, join with ss in beg 1-ch. *12 dc + twelve 1-ch sps.*

You will see the sides beg to curl up slightly.

Round 5: [1dc in next 2-ch sp, ch4] 12 times, join last 4-ch with ss in first 4-ch.

Beg to work in cont spiral. PM in first st and move up as each round is completed.

Round 6: [Ch4, 1dc in next 4-ch sp] 12 times.

Round 7: [Ch4, 1dc in next 4-ch sp, ch4, place bead dc in next 4-ch sp] 6 times.

Round 8: Rep round 6.

Round 9: Rep round 7.

Rep rounds 6 and 7 until desired height is reached.

Final round: [3dc in each 4-ch sp] to end, join with ss in first dc. *36 dc.*

Fasten off.

- Adjust the number of rounds to fit the height of the pot – smaller pots may only need a couple of rounds.

- For larger pots work more base rounds, increasing each base round by 6 stitches to keep the base flat.

- Remember the weight of the plant will pull the crochet up over the pot, so allow for this when gauging the fit.

MEDIUM POT HANGING STRANDS

Work with two strands held tog throughout.

Strand 1: Join yarn in any sp between any 3-dc group, ch1, place bead ch, [ch5, place bead ch] 8 times, ch5. Fasten off, leaving 100cm (40in) end.

Strands 2, 3 and 4: Count 9 sts from prev strand, join yarn in next sp between dc, ch1, place bead ch, [ch5, place bead ch] 8 times, ch5.

Fasten off, leaving 20cm (8in) end.

MAKING UP AND FINISHING

On the small pot, hold all four hanging strands together, making sure they are even in length (it's easy to miscount!), and join them with a big knot. Sew in the three shorter ends, leaving the 70cm (28in) end sticking out at the top. Using the 70cm (28in) end, ch12 then join with a ss in the first ch to form a hanging loop. Fasten off.

On the medium pot, knot all four hanging strands together as for the small pot, leaving the 100cm (40in) end sticking out the top. Using the 100cm (40in) end, ch20 then join with a ss in the first ch to form a hanging loop. Fasten off.

Sew in all remaining yarn ends carefully.

indian summer table mandala

As with most mandalas, some rounds are simple whilst others require full concentration – making this pattern a great tool for focusing the mind. It's very important with all mandalas to get the stitch count just right because the symmetry is based on mathematics. You can finish at any point to suit your table size.

SKILL RATING: ● ● ●

MATERIALS:
Scheepjes Cahlista (100% cotton, approx. 85m/92yds per 50g/1¾oz ball) Aran (worsted) weight yarn
1 ball each of:
    Bridal White shade 105 (A)
    Yellow Gold shade 208 (B)
    Royal Orange shade 189 (C)
    Shocking Pink shade 114 (D)
    Deep Violet shade 521 (E)
    Crystalline shade 385 (F)
    Bluebird 427 (G)

4.5mm (US size 7) crochet hook

Yarn needle

FINISHED MEASUREMENTS:
53cm (21in) diameter

TENSION (GAUGE):
Rounds 1–4 = 11.5cm (4½in) diameter, using 4.5mm (US size 7) hook.

ABBREVIATIONS:
See page 127.

SPECIAL ABBREVIATION:
edc (elongated double crochet): insert hook in st two rows below current round, yrh, pull yarn up level to current round, yrh, pull through both loops on hook to complete edc

FPhtr (front post half treble): yrh, take hook from front around post of st in previous round, yrh, pull a loop through (3 loops on hook), yrh, pull through all 3 loops

FOR THE MANDALA

Using A, ch24, join with ss in first ch to form large central ring – this needs to be large enough to comfortably fit the pole of a sun parasol.
Round 1: Ch1 (does not count as st), 32dc into the ring, join with ss in beg 1-ch. *32 sts.*
Fasten off A.
Round 2: Join B in any st, ch2 (counts as first htr throughout), 1htr in each st to end. *32 sts.*
Fasten off B.
Round 3: Join C in any st, ch2, 1htr in same st, 2htr in each st to end. *64 sts.*
Fasten off C.

Round 4: Join D in any st from round 2 and pull yarn up to level of current round, ch1 (forms first edc), ch1, *1edc in next st from round 2, ch1; rep from * in each st to end, join with ss in beg 1-ch. *32 edc + thirty-two 1-ch sps.*
Fasten off D.
Round 5: Join E in any 1-ch sp, ch1 (counts as first dc throughout), *ch3, miss next 1-ch sp, 1dc in next 1-ch sp; rep from * to last 1-ch sp, ch3, miss last 1-ch sp, join with ss in beg 1-ch. *16 dc + sixteen 1-ch sps.*
Fasten off E.
Round 6: Join F in any 3-ch sp, ch2, (1tr, ch1, 1tr, 1htr) in same 3-ch sp as join, (1htr, 1tr, ch1, 1htr, 1tr) in each 3-ch sp to end, join with ss in 2nd of beg 2-ch.
Fasten off F.

Round 7: Join A in any 1-ch sp between 2 tr, ch1, ch2, 1FPhtr in dc from round 4, ch2, *1dc in sp between 2 tr from round 6, ch2, 1FPhtr in dc from round 4, ch2; rep from * 14 times, join with ss in beg 1-ch.

Round 8: Ch3 (counts as first tr throughout), ch2, 1tr in same st, ch3, *1tr in next dc from round 7, ch2, 1tr in same st, ch3; rep from * 14 times, join with ss in 3rd of beg 3-ch.
Fasten off A.

Round 9: Join D in any 3-ch sp, ch1, (1htr, 1tr, 1dtr, ch1, 1dtr, 1tr, 1htr) in next 2-ch sp, *1dc in next 3-ch sp, (1htr, 1tr, 1dtr, ch1,1dtr, 1tr, 1htr) in next 2-ch sp; rep from * 14 times, join with ss in beg 1-ch.
Fasten off D.

Round 10: Join E in any 1-ch sp (tip of D triangle), ch1, ch6, [1dc in next 1-ch sp, ch6] 15 times, join with ss in beg 1-ch. *16 dc + sixteen 6-ch sps.*
Fasten off E.

Round 11: Join G in 6-ch sp, ch2, 7htr in same 6-ch sp, [8htr in next 6-ch sp] 15 times, join with ss in 2nd of beg 2-ch. *128 sts.*
Fasten off G.

Round 12: Join A around FP of any dc of round 10, ch2 (counts as first FPhtr), ch1, miss first st of 8-htr group, [1dc in next st, ch1, miss next st] 3 times, *1FPhtr in next dc from round 10, ch1, miss first st of 8-htr group, [1dc in next st, ch1, miss next st] 3 times; rep from * 14 times, join with ss in 2nd beg 2-ch.
Fasten off A.

Round 13: Join F in any 1-ch sp, ch2, 1htr in same sp, 2htr in each 1-ch sp to end, join with ss in 2nd of beg 2-ch.
Fasten off F.

Round 14: Join B in sp between any 2-htr group, ch1, 1dc in same sp, ch1, miss next 2 htr, [2dc in next sp between 2-htr groups, ch1, miss next 2 htr] to end, join with ss in beg 1-ch.
Fasten off B.

Round 15: Join C in any 1-ch sp, ch1, ch2, [miss next 2 dc, 1dc in next 1-ch sp, ch2] to end, join with ss in beg 1-ch. *64 dc + sixty-four 2-ch sps.*
Fasten off C.

Round 16: Join A in any 2-ch sp, ch3, ch1, 1tr in same sp, (1tr, ch1, 1tr) in each 2-ch sp to end, join with ss in 3rd of beg 3-ch. *128 tr + sixty-four 1-ch sps.*
Fasten off A.

For smaller table end here, for larger tables cont as foll:

Round 17: Join B in any 1-ch sp, ch1, ch6, [miss next 4 sts and 1-ch sp, 1dc in next 1-ch sp, ch6] to end, join with ss in beg 1-ch. *32 dc + thirty-two 6-ch sps.*
Fasten off B.

Round 18: Join C in centre of any 6-ch sp, ch1, ch7, [1dc in centre of next 6-ch sp, ch7] to end, join with ss in beg 1-ch. *32 dc + thirty-two 7-ch sps.*
Fasten off C.

Round 19: Join E in centre of any 7-ch sp, ch1, ch5, [1dc in centre of next 7-ch sp, ch5] to end, join with ss in beg 1-ch. *32 dc + thirty-two 5-ch sps.*
Fasten off E.

Round 20: Join D in any 5-ch sp, ch1, 6dc in same sp, 7dc in each 5-ch sp to end, join with ss in beg 1-ch. *224 sts.*
Fasten off D.

Round 21: Join G in any st, ch1, 1dc in each st to end, join with ss in beg 1-ch.
Fasten off G.

Round 22: Join A around FP of any dc from round 19, ch3 (counts as first FPtr), 1FPtr around same dc, [ch1, miss next st, 1dc] 3 times, miss next st, *2FPtr in next dc from round 19, [ch1, miss next st, 1dc] 3 times, miss next st; rep from * 30 times, join with ss in 3rd of beg 3-ch.
Fasten off A.

Round 23: Join F in any st, ch1, 1dc, [2dc in next 1-ch sp] 3 times, *2dc, [2dc in next 1-ch sp] 3 times; rep from * 30 times, join with ss in beg 1-ch. *256 sts.*
Fasten off F.

Round 24: Using B, ch1, 1dc in each st to end, join with ss in beg 1-ch.

Round 25: Join C in any st, ch1, ch1, miss next st, [1dc, ch1, miss next st] to end, join with ss in beg 1-ch.
Fasten off C.

Round 26: Join D in any st in round 23 that sits directly beneath 1-ch sp from round 25 and pull yarn up to level of current round, ch1 (counts as first edc), *ch1, miss next st of round 23, 1edc in next dc of round 23; rep from * to end, join with ss in beg 1-ch.
Fasten off.

MAKING UP AND FINISHING

Sew in all yarn ends carefully.

Block your work to make it into a neat circle.

light 'n' airy beaded toppers
These mandalas are an homage to my grandmother, who was always hooking a little something like this. If you are a confident beginner and have mastered the granny square you can use this project to expand your crochet repertoire and confidence.

SKILL RATING: ● ● ●

MATERIALS:
Scheepjes Catona (100% cotton, approx. 25m/27yds per 10g/⅜oz ball) 4 ply (fingering) weight yarn
1 ball each of:
    Lemon (280) (A)
    Icy Pink shade 246 (B)
    Fresia shade 519 (C)
    Bridal White shade 105 (D)
    Shocking Pink shade 114 (E)
    Sweet Orange shade 411 (F)
    Royal Orange shade 189 (G)
    Lavender shade 520 (H)

2.75mm (US size C/2) crochet hook

Yarn needle

12 beads for each cover

FINISHED MEASUREMENTS:
Small: 20cm (8in) diameter (tip to tip when blocked)
Large: 25cm (10in) diameter (tip to tip when blocked)

TENSION (GAUGE):
Rounds 1–2 = 4cm (1½in) diameter, using 2.75mm (US size C/2) hook.

ABBREVIATIONS:
See page 127.

SPECIAL ABBREVIATIONS:
4-tr cl (4-treble cluster): [yrh, insert hook in next st, pull a loop through, yrh, pull through first 2 loops on hook] 4 times (5 loops on hook), yrh, pull through all 5 loops

5-tr cl (5-treble cluster): [yrh, insert hook in ch sp, pull a loop through, yrh, pull through first 2 loops on hook] 5 times in same ch sp (6 loops on hook), yrh, pull through all 6 loops

FOR THE COVERS
SMALL COVER

Using A, make a magic ring, or ch6 and join with ss in first ch to form a ring.

Round 1: Ch1 (does not count as st throughout), 6dc into the ring, join with ss in first dc.

Round 2: Ch1, 2dc in each st around. *12 sts.*

Fasten off A, join in B.

Round 3: Ch3 (counts as first tr throughout), 1tr in same st, 2tr in each st to end. *24 sts.*

Fasten off B, join C in any st.

Round 4: Ch4 (counts as first tr and 1-ch), *1tr in next st, ch1; rep from * to end, join with ss in 3rd of beg 4-ch. *24 tr + twenty-four 1-ch sps.*

Fasten off C, join A in any 1-ch sp.

Round 5: Ch2 (counts as first dc), 1dc in same sp, 2dc in each 1-ch sp to end, join with ss in 2nd of beg 2-ch. *48 sts.*

Fasten off A, join D in any st.

Round 6: Ch3 (counts as first st of 4-tr cl), complete 4-tr cl over next 3 sts, *ch5, 4-tr cl over next 4 sts; rep from * to end, ch5, join with ss in top of first 4-tr cl. *Twelve 4-tr cl + twelve 5-ch sps.*

Fasten off D, join B in top of any 4-tr cl.

Round 7: Ch4 (counts as first tr and 1-ch), 1tr in same st, ch2, 1dc in next 5-ch sp, ch2, *(1tr, ch1, 1tr) in top of next 4-tr cl, ch2, 1dc in next 5-ch sp, ch2; rep from * to end, join with ss in 3rd of beg 4-ch.

Fasten off B, join C in any 1-ch sp from prev round.

Round 8: Ch9 (counts as first dc and 8-ch), [1dc in next 1-ch sp from prev round, ch8] 11 times, join with ss in first of beg 9-ch.

Fasten off C.

Thread 12 beads onto D, join yarn in any 8-ch sp.

Round 9: [Ch8, bring bead to hook, ch1, ss in 2nd ch from bead, ch6, 1dc in next 8-ch sp] 12 times, join with ss in first of beg 8-ch.

Fasten off.

LARGE COVER

Work rounds 1–6 as for small cover, using E for rounds 1–2, F for round 3, G for round 4, A for round 5, H for round 6.

Fasten off H, join D in any 5-ch sp from prev round.

Round 7: Ch3 (counts as first st of 5-tr cl), [yrh, insert hook in same sp, yrh, pull through 2 loops] 4 times in same sp, yrh, pull though all loops on hook (completes first 5-tr cl), ch6, 5-tr cl in next 5-ch sp, ch6; rep from * to end, join with ss in top of first 5-tr cl. *Twelve 5-tr cl + twelve 6-ch sps.*

Fasten off D, join F in top of any 5-tr cl.

Round 8: Ch5 (counts as first tr and 2-ch), 1tr in same st, ch2, 1dc in next 6-ch sp, ch2, *(1tr, ch2, 1tr) in top of next 5-tr cl, ch2, 1dc in next 6-ch sp, ch2; rep from * to end, join with ss in 3rd of 5-ch.

Fasten off F, join G in any 2-ch sp between 2-tr from prev round.

Round 9: Ch11 (counts as first dc and 10-ch), [miss next (1tr, 2-ch, 1dc, 2-ch, 1tr), 1dc in next 2-ch sp from prev round, ch10] 11 times, join with ss in first of beg 11-ch.

Fasten off G.

Thread 12 beads onto D, join yarn in any 10-ch sp.

Round 10: [Ch8, bring bead to hook, ch1, ss in 2nd ch from bead, ch6, 1dc in next 10-ch sp] 12 times, join with ss in first of beg 8-ch.

Fasten off.

MAKING UP AND FINISHING

Sew in all yarn ends carefully.

Block your work, pinning out each beaded point.

MINDFULNESS

Embrace the experience of learning and practise non-judgement. Is your intention when doing a particular pattern that it should make you feel happier and lighter? To gain a sense of achievement and fulfilment at learning something new? Whatever it is, focus on this intent and allow it to expand with every round.

granny love blanket
This blanket is a classic granny square with extra rounds to create the required size, and mini granny squares to form the border. Learning to crochet is the lifetime gift we give ourselves. It takes time and repetition to perfect, and with each stitch you work you are embedding the muscle memory.

SKILL RATING: ● ○ ○

MATERIALS:
Stylecraft Life DK (75% acrylic, 25% wool, approx. 298m/326yds per 100g/3½oz ball) DK (light worsted) weight yarn
   3 balls of Cream shade 2305 (B)
   1 ball each of:
      Heather shade 2309 (A)
      Rose shade 2301 (C)
      Lily shade 2417 (D)
      Fuchsia shade 2344 (E)

Stylecraft Tweedy (74% acrylic, 26% cotton, approx. 260m/284yds per 100g/3½oz ball) DK (light worsted) weight yarn
   1 ball of Thistle shade 3713 (F)

4.5mm (US size 7) crochet hook

Yarn needle

FINISHED MEASUREMENTS:
129cm (51in) square

TENSION (GAUGE):
Four 3-tr groups x 7 rows = 10cm (4in) square over patt, using 4.5mm (US size 7) hook.

ABBREVIATIONS:
See page 127.

SPECIAL ABBREVIATION:
edc (elongated double crochet): insert hook in st two rows below current row, yrh, pull yarn up level to current row, yrh, pull through both loops on hook to complete edc

FOR THE BLANKET

CENTRAL SQUARE

Using A, ch6 and join with ss in first ch to form a ring.

Round 1: Ch3 (counts as first tr throughout), 2tr into ring, *ch3, 3tr into the ring; rep from * twice more, join with ss in 3rd of beg 3-ch.
Fasten off A.

Round 2: Join B in any corner 3-ch sp, ch3, 2tr in same 3-ch sp (half corner made), *ch1, (3tr, ch2, 3tr) in next 3-ch sp (corner made); rep from * twice more, ch1, 3tr in same sp as beg half corner, ch2, join with ss in 3rd of beg 3-ch.
Fasten off B.

Round 3: Join C in any corner 2-ch sp, ch3, 2tr in same 2-ch sp (half corner made), *ch1, 3tr in next 1-ch sp, ch1, (3tr, ch2, 3tr) in next 2-ch sp (corner made); rep from * twice more, ch1, 3tr in next 1-ch sp, ch1, 3tr in same sp as beg half corner, ch2, join with ss in 3rd of beg 3-ch.
Fasten off C.

Round 4: Join D in any corner 2-ch sp, ch3, 2tr in same 2-ch sp (half corner made), *ch1, [3tr in next 1-ch sp, ch1] to next corner 2-ch sp, (3tr, ch2, 3tr) in 2-ch sp (corner made); rep from * twice more, ch1, [3tr in next 1-ch sp, ch1] to beg half corner, 3tr in same sp as beg half corner, ch2, join with ss in 3rd of beg 3-ch.
Fasten off D.

Round 5: Using E, rep round 4.
Round 6: Using B, rep round 4.
Round 7: Using E, rep round 4.
Round 8: Using D, rep round 4.
Round 9: Using C, rep round 4.
Round 10: Using B, rep round 4.
Round 11: Using A, rep round 4.
Round 12: Using B, rep round 4.
Round 13: Using C, rep round 4.
Round 14: Using D, rep round 4.
Rounds 15–34: Rep rounds 5–14 twice.
Round 35: Using E, rep round 4.
Rounds 36–38: Using B, rep round 4.
Fasten off.

MINI SQUARES (make 80)

Using F, ch6 and join with ss in first ch to form a ring.

Round 1: Ch3 (counts as first tr throughout), 2tr into the ring, *ch3, 3tr into the ring; rep from * twice more, join with ss in 3rd of beg 3-ch.
Fasten off F.

Join first mini square to central square using join-as-you-go method (see page 122).

MINDFULNESS

As the rounds get longer and your familiarity with the stitch and pattern deepens, you can begin the mindful journey of linking the stitch with the breath. Practise a three-part breath by breathing deeply into your belly first, then into the ribcage and finally into your upper chest. Slowly exhale, fully reversing the flow. Now practise making the out breath longer than the in breath, and use crocheting stitches as a timer. Connecting breath with movement distracts your mind and allows you to become more present.

- Where the two mini squares are joined together you will have two corner 2-ch spaces side by side. When working the border treat these two spaces as one space by working 1tr into the first space and 2tr into the next space to form the 3tr group, then ch1 to the next space.

- It can feel as if you are working into a space that is slightly backward when making the 2tr in the 2-ch sp at the base of the beginning 3ch in round 3.

Round 2: Join B in any corner 3-ch sp of mini square, ch3, 2tr in same 3-ch sp, insert hook in any 1-ch sp of central square from underneath, 1dc in 1-ch sp of central square (counts as first of 2-ch for corner sp), ch1, work second 3-tr group in same 3-ch sp of current square. Replace next 1-ch of current mini square with 1dc in next side sp of central square, 3tr in next 3-ch sp of mini square, 1dc in 1-ch sp of central square (counts as first of 2-ch for corner sp), ch1, 3tr in same 3-ch sp, *ch1, (3tr, ch2, 3tr) in next 3-ch sp (corner made); rep from * once more, ch1, join with ss in 3rd of beg 3-ch.

Cont joining squares in this way to both the central square and prev mini squares. When joining next mini square to central square and previous mini square at a shared corner, replace both corner ch of current square with 1dc in each adjoining square.

Join 80 squares to form border around central square.

FINAL BORDER

Round 1: Join B in any corner 2-ch sp, ch3 (counts as first tr throughout), 2tr in same 2-ch sp (half corner made), *work [ch1, 3tr in next 1-ch sp, ch1, work across join between mini squares with 1tr in first 2-ch sp, 2tr in next 2-ch sp] to next corner, ch1, (3tr, ch2, 3tr) in next 2-ch sp (corner made); rep from * twice, work [ch1, 3tr in next 1-ch sp, ch1, work across join between mini squares with 1tr in first 2-ch sp, 2tr in next 2-ch sp] to beg half corner, ch1, 3tr in same sp as beg half corner, ch2, join with ss in 3rd of beg 3-ch.

Round 2: Ch3, 2tr in 2-ch sp at base of 3-ch (half corner made) *ch1, [3tr in next 1-ch sp, ch1] to next corner 2-ch sp, (3tr, ch2, 3tr) in next 2-ch sp (corner made); rep from * twice more, ch1, [3tr in next 1-ch sp, ch1] to beg half corner, 3tr in same sp as beg half corner, ch2, join with ss in 3rd of beg 3-ch.
Fasten off B and rejoin B in any corner 2-ch sp.

Round 3: Ch1 (counts as first dc throughout), 1dc in each st and 1-ch sp around, working (1dc, ch2, 1dc) in each corner, ending 1dc into beg 2-ch sp, ch2, join with ss in beg 1-ch.
Fasten off B.

Round 4: Join F in any corner 2-ch sp, ch1, *[ch1, miss next st, 1edc in next st of round 2] to corner 2-ch sp, (1dc, ch2, 1dc) in corner 2-ch sp; rep from * twice more, [ch1, miss next st, 1edc in next st of round 2] to last corner 2-ch sp, 1dc in 2-ch sp, ch2, join with ss in beg 1-ch.
Fasten off.

MAKING UP AND FINISHING

Sew in all yarn ends carefully.

kaleidoscope mandala mat

Mandalas require your undivided attention because their success lies in correctly counting the stitches for each round. This makes them perfect for focusing the mind and bringing you into the present moment.

SKILL RATING: ● ● ●

MATERIALS:

Rico Essentials Cotton DK (100% cotton, approx. 130m/142yds per 50g/1¾oz ball) DK (light worsted) weight yarn

1 x ball each of:
 Royal Blue shade 36 (A)
 Fuchsia shade 14 (B)
 Natural shade 51 (C)
 Aquamarine shade 31 (D)
 Banana shade 63 (E)
 Pumpkin shade 87 (F)
 Pistachio shade 86 (G)
 Violet shade 20 (H)

3.75mm (US size F/5) crochet hook

Yarn needle

FINISHED MEASUREMENTS:

46cm (18in) diameter

TENSION (GAUGE):

Rounds 1–4 = 7cm (2¾in) diameter, using 3.75mm (US size F/5) hook.

ABBREVIATIONS:

See page 127.

SPECIAL ABBREVIATIONS:

3-tr cl (3-treble cluster): [yrh, insert hook in sp/st, yrh, pull a loop through, yrh, pull through 2 loops on hook] 3 times in same sp/st (4 loops on hook), yrh, pull though all 4 loops to complete cluster

4-tr cl (4-treble cluster): [yrh, insert hook in ch sp, yrh, pull a loop through, yrh, pull through first 2 loops on hook] 4 times in same ch sp (5 loops on hook), yrh, pull through all 5 loops to complete cluster

FPdc (front post double crochet): from front of work insert hook from right to left behind post of next st on round below and through to front again, yrh and pull loop through (2 loops on hook), yrh, pull through both loops

FOR THE MAT

MAIN MANDALA

Using A, make a magic ring, or ch6 and join with ss in first ch to form a ring.

Round 1: Ch3 (counts as first tr), 11tr into the ring, join with ss in 3rd of beg 3-ch. *12 sts.*

Fasten off A.

Round 2: Join B in any st, ch3 (counts as first tr), 1tr in same st, 2tr in each st to end, join with ss in 3rd of beg 3-ch. *24 sts.*

Fasten off B.

Round 3: Join C in any st, ch2 (counts as first dc + ch1), *1dc in next st, ch1; rep from * to end, join with ss in beg 1-ch. *24 dc + twenty-four 1-ch sps.*

Fasten off C.

Round 4: Join D in any 1-ch sp, ch2 (counts as first dc + ch1), *1dc in next 1-ch sp, ch1; rep from * to end, join with ss in first of beg 2-ch.

Fasten off D.

Round 5: Join E in any 1-ch sp, ch3 (counts as first tr), 1tr in same sp, 2tr in each 1-ch sp to end, join with ss in 3rd of beg 3-ch. *48 sts.*

Fasten off E.

Round 6: Join B in any st, ch1 (counts as first dc throughout), 1dc in each st to end, join with ss in beg 1-ch.

Fasten off B.

Round 7: Join A in any st, ch3 (counts as first dc + ch2), miss next st, *1dc in next st, ch2, miss next st; rep from * to end, join with ss in first of beg 3-ch. *24 dc + twenty-four 2-ch sps.*

Fasten off A.

Round 8: Join F in any 2-ch sp, ch3 (counts as first tr), 2tr in same sp, 3tr in each 2-ch sp to end, join with ss into 3rd of beg 3-ch. *72 sts.*

Fasten off F.

Round 9: Join C in sp between any 3-tr groups, ch2 (counts as first dc + ch1), miss next st, 1dc in next st, ch1, miss next st, *1dc in next sp between 3-tr groups, ch1, miss next st, 1dc in next st, ch1, miss next st; rep from * to end, join with ss in first of beg 2-ch. *48 dc + forty-eight 1-ch sps.*

Fasten off C.

Round 10: Join G in any 1-ch sp, ch2 (counts as first htr), 1htr in same sp, 2htr in each 1-ch sp to end, join with ss in 2nd of beg 2-ch.

Fasten off G.

Round 11: Join B in sp between any 2-htr groups, ch3 (counts as first tr of 3-tr cl), complete the 3-tr cl in same sp, ch2, miss next 2 sts, *3-tr cl in next sp between 2-htr groups, ch2, miss next 2 sts; rep from * to end, join with ss in 3rd of beg 3-ch. *Forty-eight 3-tr cl.*

Fasten off B.

Round 12: Join C in any 2-ch sp, ch1, 1dc in same 2-ch sp, 1FPdc around top of 3-tr cl, *2dc in next 2-ch sp, 1FPdc around top of next 3-tr cl; rep from * to end, join with ss in beg 1-ch. *144 sts.*

Fasten off C.

Round 13: Join D in any dc st, ch2 (counts as first dc + ch1), miss next st, *1dc in next st, ch1, miss next st; rep from * to end, join with ss in first of beg 2-ch. *72 dc + seventy-two 1-ch sps.*

Fasten off D.

Round 14: Join F in any 1-ch sp, ch1, 1dc in same sp, 2dc in each 1-ch sp to end, join with ss in beg 1-ch. *144 sts.*

Fasten off F.

Round 15: Working with B and G, join B in any st, ch2 (counts as first htr), 1htr in each of next 10 sts, change to G, 4-tr cl in next st, change to B (carrying G behind work and working over it), *1htr in each of next 11 sts, change to G, 4-tr cl in next st, change to B; rep from * to end, using B, join with ss in 2nd of beg 2-ch. *132 htr + twelve 4-tr cl.*

Fasten off B and G.

Round 16: Join F in any st, ch1, 1dc in each st to end, join with ss in beg 1-ch. *144 sts.*

Fasten off F.

Round 17: Using D, rep round 13.

Round 18: Using C, rep round 14.

Round 19: Using A, rep round 7.

Round 20: Join C in any 2-ch sp directly above 4-tr cl in round 15, ch4 (counts as first dtr), 2tr in same sp, 2htr in next 2-ch sp, 2dc in each of next two 2-ch sps, 2htr in next 2-ch sp, (2tr, 1dtr) in next 2-ch sp, ch2, *(1dtr, 2tr) in next 2-ch sp, 2htr in next 2-ch sp, 2dc in each of next two 2-ch sps, 2htr in next 2-ch sp, (2tr, 1dtr) in next 2-ch sp, ch2; rep from * to end, join with ss in 4th of beg 4-ch. *168 sts + twelve 2-ch sps.*

Fasten off C.

Round 21: Join G in any 2-ch sp, ch1, (1dc, ch2, 2dc) in same sp, 1dc in each of next 14 sts, *(2dc ch2, 2dc) in next 2-ch sp, 1dc in each of next 14 sts; rep from * to end, join with ss in beg 1-ch.

Fasten off.

MAKING UP AND FINISHING

Sew in all yarn ends carefully.

Twist strands of two different coloured yarns together and weave through rounds 2, 5 and 8 of the mat.
Twist strands of two different coloured yarns together and weave through round 2 of each mini mandala.

JOIN MINI MANDALAS TO CENTRAL MANDALA

With RS tog, place the mini mandalas alongside round 21 of the central mandala. Using G, sew together the 2 outer stitches from each mandala, starting and finishing at the 2-ch sps on round 21.

BORDER

On one mini mandala, count 6 sts up from the join at the base of the 2-ch sp from round 21.
Round 1: Join G into 6th st, ch1 (counts as first dc), 1dc in same st, *ch3, miss 3 sts, 2dc in next st; rep from * 4 times, ch1 **join to next mini mandala by working 2dc in 6th st up from join at 2-ch sp on round 21; rep from * around each mini mandala, ending last rep at **, join with ss in beg 1-ch.
Fasten off G.
Round 2: Join C in first 3-ch sp on farthest right of any mini mandala, *ch3 (counts as first tr), 5tr in same sp, [ss between next 2dc, 6tr in next 3-ch sp] 4 times, ss between last 2 dc on current mini mandala, **1dc in 1-ch sp between two mini mandalas, ss between first 2 dc of next mini mandala; rep from * to end, ending last rep at **, join with ss in 3rd of 3-ch. Fasten off.

Sew in all remaining yarn ends and block.

MINI MANDALAS (make 12—2 of each colour combination as in chart)

Using first yarn for round 1 as indicated by chart, make a magic ring, or ch6 and join with ss in first ch to form a ring.
Round 1: Ch3 (counts as first tr throughout), 11tr into ring, join with ss in 3rd of beg 3-ch. *12 sts.*
Fasten off first colour.
Round 2: Join second colour in any st, ch3, 1tr in same st, 2tr in each st to end, join with ss in 3rd of beg 3-ch. *24 sts.*
Fasten off second colour.
Round 3: Join third colour in any st, ch2 (counts as first dc + ch1), *1dc in next st, ch1; rep from * to end, join with ss in beg 1-ch. *24 dc + twenty-four 1-ch sps.*
Fasten off third colour.
Round 4: Join fourth colour in any 1-ch sp, ch2 (counts as first dc + ch1), *1dc in next 1-ch sp, ch1; rep from * to end, join with ss in beg 1-ch.
Fasten off fourth colour.
Round 5: Join fifth colour in any 1-ch sp, ch2 (counts as first htr), 1htr in same sp, 2htr in each 1-ch sp to end, join with ss in 2nd of beg 2-ch.
Fasten off.

ROUND	Mandala 1	Mandala 2	Mandala 3	Mandala 4	Mandala 5	Mandala 6
Round 1	B	H	E	B	F	D
Round 2	G	E	F	E	H	B
Round 3	C	C	C	C	C	C
Round 4	A	D	A	H	A	G
Round 5	F	B	H	F	B	H

secret garden autumn shawl

The wonderful rainbow effect of this shawl is very cheering on a dull day. There is great value to be had when working a repetitive pattern on a large project. Once the brain and hands become synchronised and a familiarity with the pattern is embedded, the mindful space is created.

SKILL RATING: ● ● ●

MATERIALS:

Scheepjes Secret Garden (60% polyester, 20% silk, approx. 93m/101yds per 50g/1¾oz ball) DK (light worsted) weight yarn
    2 balls each of:
        Rambling Blooms shade 705 (A)
        Summer House shade 707 (B)
        Secluded Lake shade 703 (C)
    1 ball of Shady Courtyard shade
        737 (D)

4.5mm (US size 7) crochet hook

Yarn needle

FINISHED MEASUREMENTS:

160cm (64in) wide x 75cm (30in) deep

TENSION (GAUGE):

14 sts x 6 rows = 10cm (4in) over treble, using 4.5mm (US size 7) hook.

ABBREVIATIONS:

See page 127.

Row 10: Rep row 5.
Rows 11 and 12: Rep row 8.
Row 13: Using B, rep row 4.
Row 14: Using A, rep row 5.
Row 15: Using B, rep row 4.
Row 16: Using A, rep row 5.
Row 17: Using A, rep row 8.
Row 18: Using B, rep row 4.
Row 19: Using A, rep row 5.
Row 20: Using A, rep row 8.
Row 21: Using B, rep row 8.
Row 22: Rep row 4.
Row 23: Rep row 5.
Row 24: Rep row 4.
Row 25: Using C, rep row 5.
Row 26: Using B, rep row 4.
Row 27: Using C, rep row 5.
Row 28: Rep row 4.
Row 29: Rep row 5.
Row 30: Rep row 4.
Row 31: Rep row 5.
Row 32: Rep row 4.
Row 33: Rep row 5.
Row 34: Using D, rep row 4.
Row 35: Rep row 5.
Row 36: Rep row 4.
Fasten off.

MAKING UP AND FINISHING

Sew in all yarn ends carefully and block to shape.

FOR THE SHAWL

Using A, make a magic ring, or ch6 and join with ss in first ch to form a ring.

Row 1: Ch3 (counts as first tr throughout), 5tr into the ring, ch2, 6tr into ring, ch2, turn. *12 sts + one 2-ch sp.*

Row 2: Ch3, 2tr in same st, 1tr in each of next 5 sts to corner 2-ch sp, (2tr, ch2, 2tr) in corner 2-ch sp, 1tr in each of next 5 sts, 3tr in top of beg 3-ch of prev row, turn. *20 sts + one 2-ch sp.*

Row 3: Ch3, 2tr in same st, 1tr in each of next 9 sts to corner 2-ch sp, (2tr, ch2, 2tr) in corner 2-ch sp, 1tr in each of next 9 sts, 3tr in top of beg 3-ch of prev row, turn. *28 sts + one 2-ch sp.*

Row 4: Ch3, 1tr in same st, ch1, 1tr in next st, *ch1, miss next st, 1tr in next st; rep from * to corner 2-ch sp (ending with 1tr in last st before corner 2-ch sp), ch1, (1tr, ch2, 1tr) in corner 2-ch sp, ch1, 1tr in next st, **ch1, miss next st, 1tr in next st; rep from ** to last st, ch1, 2tr in top of beg 3-ch of prev row, turn.

Row 5: Ch3, 2tr in same st, 1tr in next st, *1tr in next 1-ch sp, 1tr in next st; rep from * to corner 2-ch sp, (2tr, 2-ch, 2tr) in corner 2-ch sp, 1tr in next st, **1tr in next 1-ch sp, 1tr in next st; rep from ** to last st, 3tr in top of beg 3-ch of prev row, turn.

Row 6: Rep row 4.
Row 7: Rep row 5.
Row 8: Ch3, 2tr in same st, 1tr in each st to corner 2-ch sp, (2tr, ch2, 2tr) in corner 2-ch sp, 1tr in each st to last st, 3tr in top of beg 3-ch of prev row.
Row 9: Rep row 4.

● Working the 3tr into the top of the beginning 3-ch of the previous row can be quite fiddly, so you can work these last 3 stitches into the space between the posts rather than into the stitch.

● Always count the 1-ch sps on both sides in row 4 to make sure they are equal and that you haven't missed one somewhere as it is very easy to slip up on this row!

basketweave lap blanket

The lovely basketweave effect on this blanket is simply created by working three front post trebles followed by three back post trebles, and it's finished with fun pompoms at the corners. We are all different; it doesn't matter how you hold your hook or yarn, or if you don't know your Aran weight from your double knitting. All that matters is your love of crochet, the yarn and your desire to keep going.

SKILL RATING: ● ● ●

MATERIALS:

James Brett Marble Chunky (100% acrylic, approx. 312m/341yds per 200g/7oz ball) chunky (bulky) weight yarn
  2 balls each of:
    MC8 (A)
    MC44 (A)

Stylecraft Special DK (100% acrylic, approx. 295m/322yds per 100g/3½oz ball) DK (light worsted) weight yarn
  1 ball each of:
    Empire shade 1829 (B)
    Turquoise shade 1068 (B)
    Aspen shade 1422 (B)
    Bluebell shade 1082 (B)
    Teal shade 1062 (B)
    Wisteria shade 1432 (B)
    Violet shade 1277 (B)

9mm (US size M/13) crochet hook
Yarn needle
5.5cm (2¼in) pompom maker

FINISHED MEASUREMENTS:

100cm (39in) wide x 115cm (45in) long

TENSION (GAUGE):

8 tr x 3 rows = 10cm (4in) over patt, using 9mm (US size M/13) hook.

ABBREVIATIONS:

See page 127.

SPECIAL ABBREVIATION:

BPtr (back post treble): yrh, from back of work insert hook from right to left in front of post of next st on prev round and through to back again, yrh and pull a loop through, [yoh, pull through 2 loops] twice

FPtr (front post treble): yrh, from front of work insert hook from right to left behind post of next st on prev round and through to front again, yrh and pull loop through, [yrh, pull through 2 loops] twice

FOR THE BLANKET

Using one strand of any A shade and one strand of any B shade held tog, ch71.
Row 1: 1tr in 4th ch from hook (missed 3-ch counts as first tr), 1tr in each st to end, turn. *69 tr.*
Row 2: Ch3 (counts as first tr throughout), miss st at base of 3-ch, 1FPtr in each of next 2 sts, *1BPtr in each of next 3 sts, 1FPtr in each of next 3 sts; rep from * to end, turn.
Row 3: Ch3, miss st at base of 3-ch, 1BPtr in each of next 2 sts, *1FPtr in each of next 3 sts, 1BPtr in each of next 3 sts; rep from * to end, turn.
Row 4: Ch3, miss st at base of 3-ch, 1BPtr in each of next 2 sts, *1FPtr in each of next 3 sts, 1BPtr in each of next 3 sts; rep from * to end, turn.
Row 5: Ch3 (counts as first tr throughout), miss st at base of 3-ch, 1FPtr in each of next 2 sts, *1BPtr in each of next 3 sts, 1FPtr in each of next 3 sts; rep from * to end, turn.
Rows 6–69: Rep rows 2–5.
Fasten off.

MAKING UP AND FINISHING

Sew in all yarn ends carefully.

POMPOMS
Using a mix of B yarns, make four 5.5cm (2¼in) pompoms. Sew a pompom to each corner of the blanket.

> ● Work with two strands held together throughout, one Marble Chunky colour and one Special DK colour.
>
> ● Change one yarn colour at a time, aiming for a colour change every row.

MINDFULNESS

Learn from others but do not be put off – you are your own teacher. Follow your heart with this blanket: trust the colour blends you choose and as you crochet allow yourself to fully relax into the rhythmical flow of working into the posts. This is a physical activity where the mind and body can harmonise.

chapter 4
caring and sharing

retro flower garland

A single flower makes a lovely gift presented on a card, or they can be strung together as a summer flower garland. Each is simple to make and they are great for the confident beginner to take the next step with their crochet. Work slowly until you are familiar with this yarn as it can sometimes split a little.

SKILL RATING: ● ● ●

MATERIALS:

Scheepjes Cahlista (100% cotton, approx. 85m/92yds per 50g/1¾oz ball) Aran (worsted) weight yarn

⅓ ball each of:
Lime Juice shade 392
Shocking Pink shade 114
Lavender shade 520
Bridal White shade 105
Yellow Gold shade 208

4mm (US size G/6) crochet hook

Yarn needle

FINISHED MEASUREMENTS:

132cm (52in) long

TENSION (GAUGE):

Sunflower = 7.5cm (3in) diameter, using 4mm (US size G/6) hook.

ABBREVIATIONS:

See page 127.

SPECIAL ABBREVIATION:

edc (elongated double crochet): insert hook in st two rows below current row, yrh, pull yarn up level to current row, yrh, pull through both loops on hook to complete edc

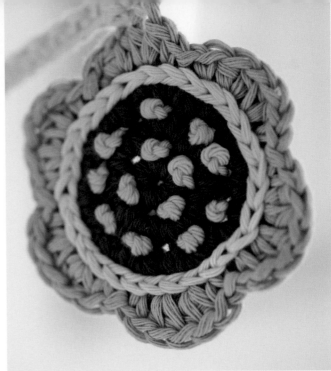

FOR THE GARLAND

Use any colour in any combination.

SMALL 5-PETAL BLOSSOM (make 8)

Using first colour, make a magic ring, or ch6 and join with ss in first ch to form a ring.

Round 1: Ch1 (does not count as st throughout), 10dc into the ring. *10 sts.*
Fasten off.

Round 2: Join second colour in any st, *(1htr, 1tr, 1htr) in next st, ss in next st; rep from * 4 times.
5 petals.
Fasten off.

SUNFLOWER (make 3)

Using first colour, make a magic ring, or ch6 and join with ss in first ch to form a ring.

Round 1: Ch1 (does not count as st throughout), 10dc into the ring, join with ss in beg 1-ch. *10 sts.*

Round 2: Ch1, 2dc in each st to end, join with ss in first dc. *20 sts.*

Round 3: Ch1, [1dc in next st, 2dc in next st] 10 times, join with ss in first dc. *30 sts.*
Fasten off.

Round 4: Join second colour in any st, *1dc in next st, (1htr, 1tr) in next st, (1tr, 1htr) in next st, 1dc in next st, ss in next st; rep from * 5 times. *6 petals.*
Fasten off.

Each flower pattern can be
worked in isolation, so they are
great for making in a spare five
minutes to soothe your mind –
just like taking a mini break.

LARGE 7-PETAL FLOWER (make 4)

Using first colour, make a magic ring, or ch6 and join with ss in first ch to form a ring.

Round 1: Ch1 (does not count as st throughout), 7dc into the ring. *7 sts.*

Round 2: Ch1, 2dc in each st to end, join with ss in first dc. *14 sts.*
Fasten off.

Round 3: Join second colour in any st, ch1, [1dc in next st, 2dc in next st] 7 times, join with ss in first dc. *21 sts.*
Fasten off.

Round 4: Join third colour in second dc of any 2-dc inc in round 2, pull yarn up to level of current round, ch1 (counts as 1dc), *ch5, miss next 2 sts, 1edc in second dc of next 2-dc inc in round 2 (ensuring you bring yarn up to level of current round); rep from * 5 times, ch5, miss last 2 sts, join with ss in beg 1-ch. *7 petals.*

Round 5: *5dc in next 5-ch sp, ss in top loop of edc from round 4; rep from * to end, join with ss in last edc.
Fasten off.

MAKING UP AND FINISHING

To add embellishments to the sunflower, with RS facing and using any contrasting colour, work a round of surface crochet (see page 126) around the outer edge of round 3. Cut the yarn and thread it through the last stitch to fasten off, then thread the end onto a yarn needle. Insert the needle into the first stitch – the same place as if you were crocheting this stitch – and pull through. Then insert the needle into the back loop of the previous stitch and pull through to make an invisible join in the circle of surface crochet. To finish, sew in the end.

With RS facing and using any contrasting colour in a yarn needle, make 5 French knots (see page 123) between the stitches in round 1 and 10 French knots in the stitches between rounds 2 and 3.

To assemble the garland, using pale green, ch15, join with a ss in 15th ch from hook to form hanging loop, *ch10, join a small petal blossom by working 1dc in any st, ch10, join a large 7-petal flower by working 1dc in each of the top two sts of any petal, ch10, join a small petal blossom by working 1dc in any st, ch10, join sunflower by working 1dc in each of the 2 tr sts of any petal; rep from * until all flowers are joined ending with a small petal blossom, ch25, join with a ss in 15th ch from hook to form hanging loop. With WS facing and working back down ch, ch1, 1dc in each ch to first hanging loop.
Fasten off.

Sew in all yarn ends carefully.

summer sun coasters

Simple and quick to make, each coaster is designed to make the colours sing no matter which combination you choose. Repeat the pattern using a different colour for each round and notice which combination makes you happiest! If you've mastered the treble crochet stitch and can make a simple circle, then this project is the perfect next step.

SKILL RATING: ● ● ●

MATERIALS:

Scheepjes Cahlista (100% cotton, approx. 85m/92yds per 50g/1¾oz ball) Aran (worsted) weight yarn
  1 ball each of:
    Sweet Orange shade 411
    Shocking Pink shade 114
    Crystalline shade 385
    Light Orchid shade 226
    Old Lace shade 130

4.5mm (US size 7) crochet hook

Yarn needle

FINISHED MEASUREMENTS:

11.5cm (4½in) diameter

TENSION (GAUGE):

Exact tension (gauge) is not important on this project.

ABBREVIATIONS:

See page 127.

SPECIAL ABBREVIATION:

edc (elongated double crochet): insert hook in st two rows below current row, yrh, pull yarn up level to current row, yrh, pull through both loops on hook to complete edc

FOR THE COASTERS

Use any sequence of colours.
Using first colour, make a magic ring, or ch6 and join with ss in first ch to form a ring.
Round 1: Ch2 (counts as first htr throughout), 11htr into the ring, join with ss in 2nd of beg 2-ch. *12 sts.*
Fasten off.
Round 2: Join second colour in any st, ch2, 1htr in same sp, 2htr in next and each st to end, join with ss in 2nd of beg 2-ch. *24 sts.*
Fasten off.
Round 3: Join third colour in any sp between 2 htr in prev round, ch2, 2htr in same sp, *miss next 2 htr, 3htr in next sp between 2 htr in prev round; rep from * to end, join with ss in 2nd of beg 2-ch. *36 sts.*
Fasten off.

● Work slowly through the stitches as Aran (worsted) weight cotton can split a little if you rush it.

● After round 4 your work may feel a little floppy around the edges, but the next two rounds will tighten it all up and bring it together to lie flat.

Round 4: Join fourth colour in second htr of any 2-htr group in round 2, pull yarn level to new round, ch1 (counts as first edc), *miss first htr of 3-htr group in prev round, 1dc in each of next 2 sts, 1edc in second htr of next 2-htr group in round 2; rep from * to end, finishing last rep with 1dc in each of last 2 sts, join with ss in beg 1-ch. *12 edc + 24 dc.*
Fasten off.

Round 5: Join fifth colour in any st in prev round, ch1 (counts as first dc), 1dc in each st to end, join with ss in beg 1-ch.
Fasten off.

Round 6: Join first colour in any st above edc in round 4, ch2 (counts as first htr), (1htr, ch2, 2htr) in same st, *miss 2 sts, (2htr, ch2, 2htr) in next st; rep from * to end, join with ss in 2nd of beg 2-ch. *48 htr + twelve 2-ch sps.*
Fasten off.

MAKING UP AND FINISHING

Sew in all yarn ends carefully.

tea light holder cover

Working with a small hook and a fine yarn requires little strength but expert dexterity and a focused mind. Take it slow to begin with, as working into the foundation chain is the trickiest bit. Perfect this and the rest becomes easy! Once complete the candlelight will flicker through the open stitches like sunlight through stained glass. This pattern can easily be adjusted for any size candle holder.

SKILL RATING: ● ● ○

MATERIALS:
Hedgehog Fibres Sock Yarn (90% merino wool, 10% nylon, approx. 400m/437yds per 100g/3½oz hank) 4 ply (fingering) weight yarn
   Small amount each of:
      Villain (A)
      Heyday (B)

2.5mm (US size B/1–C/2) crochet hook

Yarn needle

FINISHED MEASUREMENTS:
Cover: 5.5cm (2¼in) high, 19cm (7½in) circumference, to fit a tea light holder 6.5cm (2½in) diameter

TENSION (GAUGE):
Exact tension (gauge) is not important on this project – the foundation chain should be an even number of chain and fit snugly around the base.

ABBREVIATIONS:
See page 127.

SPECIAL ABBREVIATION:
PC (4-tr popcorn): work 4tr all in same st, remove hook from loop and insert in top of first tr made, pick up dropped loop again, yrh and join with a ss, pull tight so popcorn pops forward

- The container can be an old jam jar or tea light holder, but the sides must be straight and not taper too much.

- Keep fitting your work over your tea light holder to ensure a snug fit. If it's too loose, reduce the number of foundation chain.

- The best yarn is a 4 ply or fingering weight, as we want the candlelight to shine through.

- Stay fire-safe by ensuring that your crochet does not go over the top of your candle holder.

FOR THE COVER

Using A, ch40, making sure ch is not twisted, join with ss in first ch.

Round 1: Ch1, 1dc in each ch to end, ss in first ch to join. *40 sts.*

Round 2: Ch3 (counts as first tr), 1tr in each st to end, join with ss in 3rd of beg 3-ch.

Round 3: Rep round 2.

Round 4: Ch4 (counts as 1tr and ch1 throughout), *miss next st, 1tr, ch1; rep from * to end, join with ss in 3rd of beg 4-ch. *20 tr + twenty 1-ch sps.*

Round 5: Rep round 4.

Fasten off A.

Round 6: Join B with ss in any 1-ch sp, ch3 (counts as first tr of PC), complete PC in same sp, *ch3, miss next 1-ch sp, PC in next 1-ch sp; rep from * to last 1-ch sp, ch3, miss last 1-ch sp, join with ss in 3rd of beg 3-ch. *10 PC + ten 3-ch sps.*

Fasten off B.

Round 7: Join A in top of any PC, ch4, [1tr in next 3-ch sp, ch1, 1tr in top of next PC, ch1] 9 times 1tr in last 3-ch sp, ch1, join with ss in 3rd of beg 4-ch. *20 tr + twenty 1-ch sps.*

Round 8: Ch4, miss next st, [1tr, ch1, miss next st] 19 times. *20 tr + twenty 1-ch sps.*

Fasten off A.

For taller candle holder, rep rows 6–8 to desired height.

Round 9: Join B in any 1-ch sp, ch1 (counts as first dc), (1htr, 1tr) in same sp, (1tr, 1htr, 1dc) in next 1-ch sp, *(1dc, 1htr, 1tr) in next 1-ch sp, (1tr, 1htr, 1dc) in next 1-ch sp; rep from * 8 times, join with ss in beg 1-ch. *10 scallops.*

Fasten off.

MAKING UP AND FINISHING

Sew in all yarn ends carefully.

heart garland

Take a few minutes out of your hectic day to make a little heart to give as a gift, or string several together to make a pretty garland for your window or shelf. Each heart takes 10 minutes, so gives you the satisfaction of completing a make in one sitting – perfect if you are sat in a waiting room or at a bus stop. You will need to be confident with treble crochet and working in the round.

SKILL RATING: ● ● ○

MATERIALS:

Scheepjes Catona (100% cotton, approx. 25m/27yds per 10g/⅜oz ball) 4 ply (fingering) weight yarn
  1 ball each of:
    Icy Pink shade 246
    Lilac Mist shade 399
    Fresia shade 519
    Crystalline shade 385

3.5mm (US size E/4) crochet hook

Yarn needle

FINISHED MEASUREMENTS:

99cm (39in) long

TENSION (GAUGE):

One heart = 7cm (2¼in) wide, using 3.5mm (US size E/4) hook.

ABBREVIATIONS:

See page 127.

SPECIAL ABBREVIATION:

MP (make picot): ch2, join with ss in front 2 loops of tr at base of 2-ch

MINDFULNESS

Tie a heart somewhere visible for a complete stranger to enjoy – this could be the act that makes the difference in their day; a mini yarn bomb spreading the yarn love far and wide.

FOR THE GARLAND

HEARTS (make 8)

Using first colour, make a magic ring, or ch6 and join with ss in first ch to form a ring.

Round 1: Ch1 (does not count as st throughout), 10htr into the ring, join with ss in first htr. *10 sts.*

Round 2: Ch3, miss st at base of 3-ch, (1tr, 2dtr) in next st, 2tr in next st, 1htr in next st, 2dc in next st, (2tr, MP, 1tr) in next st, 2dc in next st, 1htr in next st, 2tr in next st, (2dtr, 1tr) in next st, ch3, join with ss in same st.
Fasten off.

Round 3: Join second colour in picot, ch2, 1dc in each of next 6 sts, 2dc in each of next 3 sts, 3dc in 3-ch sp, ss in middle st between two 3-ch, 3dc in next 3-ch sp, 2dc in each of next 3 sts, 1dc in each of next 6 sts, (1dc, 1htr) in picot, join with ss in beg 2-ch.
Fasten off.

MAKING UP AND FINISHING

Using any colour, ch15, join with ss in 15th ch from hook to form hanging loop, ch10, *with heart RS facing work 1dc in each dc of top 2-dc inc of first heart 'peak', ch6, miss 6 sts on heart, 1dc in each dc of top 2-dc inc of 2nd heart 'peak', ch6; rep from * until all hearts are joined, finishing with 25ch, join with ss in 15th ch from hook to form hanging loop, turn.

With WS facing and working back down ch, ch1, 1dc in each ch to join of first hanging loop. Fasten off.

Sew in all yarn ends carefully.

stress ball key ring charm

Squeeze away the stress with these pocket size mini stress balls. Put them on your key ring as here, or tie them to your bag, and you'll have your stress ball with you wherever you are! Anything goes when choosing the colour combinations of your little crochet circles – so have fun and be playful. The pattern is for four stress balls.

SKILL RATING: ● ● ○

MATERIALS:

Rico Ricorumi DK (100% cotton, approx. 58m/63yds per 25g/⅞oz ball) DK (light worsted) weight yarn

1 ball each of:
- White shade 001
- Raspberry shade 013
- Orange shade 027
- Lilac shade 017
- Purple shade 020
- Yellow shade 006
- Tangerine shade 026
- Blue shade 032
- Sky Blue shade 031
- Grass Green shade 044
- Light Green shade 046
- Emerald shade 042

3.75mm (US size F/5) crochet hook

Polyester toy filling

Yarn needle

Key ring or bag charm fixing

10cm (4in) wide piece of card

Assorted beads

FINISHED MEASUREMENTS:

7.5cm (3in) diameter, not including tassel

TENSION (GAUGE):

Exact tension (gauge) is not important on this project.

ABBREVIATIONS:

See page 127.

SPECIAL ABBREVIATION:

edc (elongated double crochet): insert hook in st two rounds below current round, yrh, pull yarn up level to current round, yrh, pull through both loops on hook to complete edc

MAKING UP AND FINISHING

Using any colour, work surface crochet (see page 126) around rounds 1 and 3 of each circle.
Fasten off and sew in yarn ends.

JOIN THE CIRCLES

Hold two circles with WS tog, matching the corresponding edge stitches. Using any colour, work a double crochet seam (see page 124) to join, working 2dc in every fourth st. Stuff with polyester toy filling when about three-quarters of the way around, then complete the seam and join with a ss in the 1-ch.
Fasten off, leaving a 25cm (10in) end.
Rep to make up the other three stress balls.

ADD THE KEY RING/BAG CHARM FITTING

Using the 25cm (10in) end, ch2, remove the hook from the loop and push the loop through the key ring eyelet, replace the loop on the hook, ch2, join with a ss in the base of the ch.
Fasten off.

Sew in all yarn ends carefully.

ADD A TASSEL OR POMPOM

Using any combination of yarn colours, wrap yarn thickly around a 10cm (4in) piece of card. Cut a 25cm (10in) length of yarn, slide it under the strands and tie in a knot at the top. Remove the tassel from the card, and bind it securely just below the top, using a contrasting colour of yarn. Thread some beads onto the ends at the top, then use the remaining yarn end to sew the tassel onto the stress ball.

Alternatively make a small pompom (see page 125) using any combination of yarn colours. Leave a 20cm (8in) end at the top, thread on some beads then use to sew the pompom onto the stress ball directly opposite and central to the key ring fixing.

FOR THE BAUBLE

CIRCLES (make 8 in assorted colours)

Using first colour, ch6, join with ss in first ch to form a ring.
Round 1: Ch3 (counts as first tr), 11tr into the ring, join with ss into 3rd of beg 3-ch. *12 sts*.
Fasten off first colour.
Round 2: Join second colour in any st, ch2 (counts as htr), 1htr in same st, 2htr in each st to end, join with ss in 2nd of beg 2-ch. *24 sts.*
Fasten off second colour.
Round 3: Join third colour in any st from round 1 and pull yarn up level to current round, ch1 (counts as first edc), 1dc in next st, *1edc in next st, 1dc in next st; rep from * to end, join with ss in beg 1-ch.
Fasten off third colour.
Round 4: Join fourth colour in any st, ch1 (counts as first dc), 1dc in same st (inc), 1dc in each of next 2 sts, *2dc in next st, 1 dc in each of next 2 sts; rep from * to end, join with ss in beg 1-ch.
Fasten off fourth colour.

MINDFULNESS

When we express gratitude for the blessings in our lives, when our mind turns toward these things, our hearts open up. It's a beautiful thing to give a handmade piece of crochet to someone as a gift. The very act of making and giving expands our lives and touches the life of the recipient, too.

flowers in a bobbin

Say it with flowers! No matter what is happening in your life, there is always something or someone to be grateful for. Express your love and gratitude to someone special and observe your life expanding. As you crochet really think about the person who will be receiving the flower you are making, and infuse every stitch with the gratitude you have for their contribution to your life. The touch and feel of these delicate yarns is a sensory pleasure and if, like me, you need to rest your mind from chronic pain then making these flowers may just take the edge off.

SKILL RATING: ● ● ○

MATERIALS:

Scheepjes Alpaca Rhythm (80% alpaca, 20% wool, approx. 200m/218yds per 25g/⅞oz ball) lace weight yarn
  1 ball of Bop shade 670 (A)

Scheepjes Mohair Rhythm (70% mohair, 30% microfibre, approx. 200m/218yds per 25g/⅞oz ball) lace weight yarn
  1 ball of Bop shade 690 (A)

Hedgehog Fibres Sock Yarn (90% merino wool, 10% nylon, approx. 400m/437yds per 100g/3½oz hank) 4 ply (fingering) weight yarn
  1 ball each of:
    Banana Legs (B)
    Birthday Cake (B)
    Villain (B)

Scheepjes Catona (100% cotton, approx. 25m/27yds per 10g/⅜oz ball) 4 ply (fingering) weight yarn
  1 ball of Apple Granny shade 513 (C)

3mm (US size C/2–D/3) and 2.5mm (US size B/1–C/2) crochet hooks

Yarn needle

Florist or garden wire

Large wooden bobbin for display

FINISHED MEASUREMENTS:

Flower: approx. 6.5cm (2½in) diameter

TENSION (GAUGE):

Exact tension (gauge) is not important on this project.

ABBREVIATIONS:

See page 127.

FOR THE FLOWER

FLOWER HEAD

With both A strands held tog and using a 3mm (US size C/2–D/3) hook, make a magic ring, or ch6 and join with ss in first ch to form a ring.
Round 1 (RS): Ch2 (counts as first htr), 11htr into the ring, join with ss in beg 2-ch. *12 sts*.
Round 2: Ch1 (counts as first dc), [ch2, miss next st, 1dc in next st] 5 times, ch2, miss last st, join with ss in beg 1-ch.
Fasten off.
Round 3 (petals): Using 2.5mm (US size B/1–C/2) hook, join any B yarn with ss in any 2-ch sp, [(ch5, 3ttr, ch5, ss) in same 2-ch sp, ss in next 2-ch sp] 6 times. *6 petals*.
Fasten off.

LEAVES (make 2 per stem)

Using C and 2.5mm (US size B/1–C/2) hook, leaving a 10cm (4in) end, ch8, ss in 2nd ch from hook, ss in next ch, 1dc in next ch, 1htr in next ch, 1tr in next ch, 1htr in next ch, (1dc, ch1, 1dc) in last ch, working back along opposite side of ch, 1htr in next ch, 1tr in next ch, 1htr in next ch, 1dc in next ch, ss in next ch.
Fasten off.

STEM (make 1 per flower head)

Cut wire to desired length allowing 5cm (2in) extra to attach to flower. Bend wire at top into small loop.
Using C and 2.5mm (US size B/1–C/2) hook, ss to base of wire, work dc around the wire to roughly midpoint (or earlier), use long end to tie leaf securely in place, pulling it tightly to ensure leaf does not flop down. Cont to dc around the wire, adding second leaf and working over leaf ends to secure them as you go.
Fasten off.

MAKING UP AND FINISHING

Sew in all yarn ends carefully.

With the RS facing outward, and using A, sew the flower head to the wire loop at the top of the stem. Bend the last 5cm (2in) of the wire and push into the bobbin.

flower power desk tidy

I love the simplicity of this little project. Each of the component pieces can be made in a single sitting, and with a colour change on every round you can pick and choose to suit your mood. I like to make all the circles first just because they look pretty when I line them all up! This is a lovely 'next step' project for beginners, to stretch their crochet abilities beyond the classic granny square. By practising new stitches and patterns you overcome your limitations and move beyond them, expanding your crochet and confidence.

SKILL RATING: ● ● ●

MATERIALS:

Scheepjes Cahlista (100% cotton, approx. 85m/92yds per 50g/1¾oz ball) Aran (worsted) weight yarn
½ ball each of:
   Jet Black shade 110 (MC)
   Crystalline shade 385
   Delphinium shade 113
   Shocking Pink shade 114
   Royal Orange shade 189
   Yellow Gold shade 208

4.5mm (US size 7) crochet hook

Yarn needle

25 x 35cm (10 x 14in) of black felt fabric

Sewing needle and black thread

Colourful embroidery thread

FINISHED MEASUREMENTS:

11.5cm (4½in) wide, 11.5cm (4½in) deep

TENSION (GAUGE):

Rounds 1–2 = 6.5cm (2½in) diameter, using 4.5mm (US size 7) hook.

ABBREVIATIONS:

See page 127.

FOR THE DESK TIDY

CIRCLE IN A SQUARE (make 5)

Using first colour, make a magic ring, or ch6 and join with ss in first ch to form a ring.
Round 1: Ch3 (counts as first tr throughout), 11tr into the ring, join with ss in 3rd of beg 3-ch. *12 sts.*
Fasten off first colour.
Round 2: Join second colour in any st, ch3, 1tr in same st, 2tr in each st to end, join with ss in 3rd of beg 3-ch. *24 sts.*
Fasten off second colour.
Round 3: Join third colour in sp between any 2-tr group in round 2, ch3, 2tr in same sp, [miss next 2 sts, 3tr in next sp between tr] 11 times, miss last 2 sts, join with ss in 3rd of beg 3-ch. *36 sts.*
Fasten off third colour.
Round 4: Join MC in sp between any 3-tr group in round 3, working in sps between 3-tr groups throughout, ch3, (2tr, ch2, 3tr) all in same sp (corner), *3htr in each of next 2 sps, (3tr, ch2, 3tr) in next sp (corner); rep from * twice, 3htr in each of last 2 sps, join with ss in 3rd of beg 3-ch.
Fasten off MC.

MAKING UP AND FINISHING

Place one square as the centre base square and arrange the other squares with one on each side to form a cross shape. Take the base square and one side square and holding the two squares with WS together, join a contrasting colour yarn into corner and ch1. Work a double crochet seam (see page 124) to join the two pieces, working through the inside loop only of each corresponding stitch. Fasten off, then repeat to join the other three squares to the sides of the base square.

Using a different coloured yarn for each side seam, join each pair of adjacent squares with a double crochet seam to make an open-topped cube.

ADD THE LINING

Measure the internal sides of the crochet cube and cut five squares of felt to match. Using the sewing needle and black thread, oversew (see page 124) the felt squares together to make a lining for the crochet cube. Using the sewing needle and bright embroidery thread, work 13 blanket stitches per side around the top edge of the felt cube.

Push the felt cube inside the crochet cube with WS together. Join any colour yarn in corner sp of any crochet square, then work 1dc into each stitch and each blanket stitch to join the two cubes together (13 stitches per side).
Fasten off and sew in all yarn ends carefully.

MINDFULNESS

This is a good little project if you need to take a 5-minute breather, because the small circles demand little of us beyond choosing the next colour. Once you have mastered the pattern you can sit and make the circles without any thought needed, allowing your mind to gently wander as your hand guides the hook through the yarn.

● Using black as the base colour really brings out the other bright shades, but you may want to work round 4 in good natural light.

prayer beads purse

This super-bright purse is made from hexagons and half hexagons, using up small scraps of yarn. Follow the layout diagram when joining the pieces as you go, to create the correct shape.

MINDFULNESS

The greatest gift from my practise of Buddhism has been the transformative experience of having and expressing gratitude. Making this purse as a gift is an act of love and generosity, as it represents many hours of crochet time and care. When we give to others it comes back to us in the form of raised self-esteem, self-worth and happiness. Give your crochet creations to those you are grateful to, and your heart and life will expand.

SKILL RATING: ● ● ●

MATERIALS:

Scheepjes Catona (100% cotton, approx. 25m/27yds per 10g/⅜oz ball) 4 ply (fingering) weight yarn
  1 ball each of:
    Ultra Violet shade 282
    Jade shade 514
    Midnight shade 527
    Cyan shade 397
    Crystalline shade 385
    Lime Juice shade 392
    Yellow Gold shade 208
    Royal Orange shade 189
    Tulip shade 222
    Shocking Pink shade 114

Scheepjes Catona (100% cotton, approx. 62.5m/68yds per 25g/⅞oz ball) 4 ply (fingering) weight yarn
  1 ball of Bridal White shade 105 (A)

3.5mm (US size E/4) crochet hook

Yarn needle

2cm (¾in) button

FINISHED MEASUREMENTS:

20cm (8in) wide x 11.5cm (4½in) deep (when closed)

TENSION (GAUGE):

Rounds 1–4 of hexagon = 4.5cm (1¾in), using 3.5mm (US size E/4) hook.

ABBREVIATIONS:

See page 127.

FOR THE PURSE

Work join-as-you-go method (see page 122), following the diagram on page 109 for placement.

STARTER HEXAGON (MAKE 1)
Using any colour, make a magic ring, or ch6 and join with ss in first ch to form a ring.
Round 1: Ch2 (counts as 1htr), 11htr into ring, join with ss in 2nd of beg 2-ch. *12 sts.*
Fasten off first colour.
Round 2: Join second colour in any st, ch1 (counts as first dc), 1dc in same st, ch1, miss next st, [2dc in next st, ch1, miss next st] 5 times, join with ss in beg 1-ch. *12 sts + six 1-ch sps.*
Fasten off second colour.
Round 3: Join third colour in any 1-ch sp, ch2 (counts as 1dc + ch1), 1dc in same sp (first corner), ch1, [(1dc, ch1, 1dc) in next 1-ch sp (for corner), ch1] 5 times, join with ss in first of beg 2-ch. *12 sts + twelve 1-ch sps.*
Fasten off third colour.
Round 4: Join fourth colour in any corner 1-ch sp, ch3 (counts as first dc + ch2 throughout), 1dc in same sp (first corner), [2dc in next 1-ch sp, (1dc, ch2, 1dc) in next 1-ch sp (for corner)] 5 times, 2dc in next 1-ch sp, join with ss in first of beg 3-ch.
Fasten off.

● **Change colour on every round throughout.**

NEXT AND SUBSEQUENT HEXAGONS (make 22)

Rounds 1–3: As for starter hexagon.

Round 4: Join fourth colour in any corner 1-ch sp, ch3, 1dc in same sp (first corner), 2dc in next 1-ch sp, 1dc in next corner 1-ch sp, then instead of ch2 for next corner sp, insert hook in corner sp of starting hexagon from underneath, 1dc in corner sp of starting hexagon (counts as first of 2-ch for corner sp), ch1, work second dc in corner sp of current hexagon, 1dc in next st in starter hexagon, 2dc in next 1-ch sp of current hexagon, miss next st on starter hexagon, 1dc in starter hexagon, miss next st on current hexagon, 1dc in next corner 2-ch sp on current hexagon, 1dc in corner 2-ch sp of starter hexagon, ch1, 1dc in same 2-ch sp of current hexagon.
Cont around to finish round 4 of current hexagon as normal.

Cont to join hexagons in this way throughout, according to the diagram opposite (page 109). When joining a hexagon to two previous hexagons at shared corners, join as above but replace both corner ch of current hexagon with 1dc in each adjoining hexagon.

HALF HEXAGON (make 4)

Worked in rows.
Using any colour, make a magic ring.

Row 1: Ch2 (counts as 1htr), 5htr into ring, turn. *6 sts.*
Fasten off first colour.

Row 2: Join second colour in first st, ch2 (counts as 1dc throughout), 2dc in next st, [ch1, miss next st, 2dc] twice working last 2dc in 2nd of beg 2-ch from row 1, turn. *7 sts + two 1-ch sps.*
Fasten off second colour.

Row 3: Join third colour in first st, ch2, 1dc in st at base of 2-ch, ch1, [(1dc, ch1, 1dc) in 1-ch sp (corner), ch1] twice, 2dc in last st (2nd of beg 2-ch from prev row), turn. *8 sts + five 1-ch sps.*
Fasten off third colour.

Row 4: Join fourth colour in first st, ch2, 1dc in st at base of 2-ch, [2dc in next 1-ch sp, (1dc, ch2, 1dc) in next corner 1-ch sp] twice, 2dc in next 1-ch sp, 2dc in last st (2nd of beg 2-ch from prev row). *14 sts + two 2-ch sps.*
Fasten off.

DIAMOND

Worked in rows.
Using any colour, make a magic ring.

Row 1: Ch2 (counts as 1htr), 3htr into ring, turn. *4 sts.*
Fasten off first colour.

Row 2: Join second colour in first st, ch2 (counts as 1dc throughout), 2dc in next st, ch1, miss next st, 2dc in last st (2nd of beg 2-ch from prev row), turn.
Fasten off second colour.

Row 3: Join third colour in first st, ch2, 1dc in st at base of 1-ch, ch1, (1dc, ch1, 1dc) in 1-ch sp (corner), ch1, 2dc in last st (2nd of beg 2-ch from prev row), turn.
Fasten off second colour.

Row 4: Join fourth colour in first st, ch2, 1dc in st at base of 1-ch, ch1, 2dc in next 1-ch sp, (1dc, ch2, 1dc) in next corner 1-ch sp (corner), 2dc in next 1-ch sp, ch1, 2dc in last st (2nd of beg 2-ch from prev row).
Fasten off.

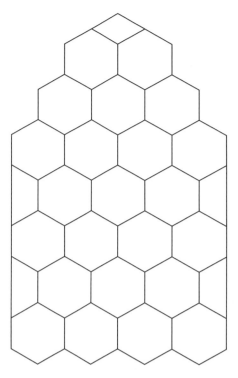

MAKING UP AND FINISHING

Sew in all yarn ends carefully.

Sew the half hexagons into position at either end of the second and fourth rows from the bottom, using whip stitch (see page 125).

Sew the diamond between the two hexagons on the top row, with the magic ring at the top.

Lay the work flat with RS facing.

BORDER

Round 1: Join A in bottom right corner hexagon on row 1, ch1 (counts as 1dc throughout), 1dc in each of next 5 sts along side of hexagon, 1dc per row along first side of half hexagon (4 sts), 1dc in magic ring centre, 1dc per row along second side of half hexagon (9 sts total along half hexagon).
Cont to work dc border around as set to diamond, work 1dc per row along first side of diamond to magic ring point (4 sts), ch5, 1dc per row along second side of diamond.
Cont to work dc border around as set to end, join with ss in beg 1-ch.
Round 2: Ch1, 1dc in each st to 5-ch at tip, 5dc in 5-ch sp, 1dc in each st to end, join with ss in beg 1-ch. Fasten off.

MAKING UP THE PURSE

With WS together, fold the piece in half aligning the bottom row to the fifth row. Using the yarn needle and A, sew the first side seam together, joining the back loops with whip stitch. Rep for the second side seam.

Turn the purse RS out and sew a button into position to fit the 5-ch buttonhole space.

christmas baubles

I'm in love with these little baubles, and when they emerged from my hook my heart skipped a beat! They make the perfect Christmas gift to give to the people we love and value in our lives. The French knot is a wonderful embellishment – and if you have yet to master it watch out, because once you do you will be placing them on everything!

MINDFULNESS

Crochet is a wonderful way to meet new like-minded people and I encourage you to seek out your local knitting and crochet group. Sharing our love of crochet with others, whilst hooking handmade gifts for friends or charity, expands our hearts and our lives. If you struggle with loneliness let crochet be a way of connecting with others. Never underestimate the power of the hook to bring people together.

SKILL RATING: ● ● ○

MATERIALS:

For the circles:
Rico Creative Cotton Aran (100% cotton, approx. 85m/92yds per 50g/1¾oz ball) Aran (worsted) weight yarn
  Small amount each of:
    Banana shade 68
    Violet shade 16
    Rose shade 00
    Light green shade 40
    Sky Blue shade 37
    Candy shade 64
    Tangerine shade 76
    Orange shade 74
    Emerald shade 69
    Cardinal shade 11
    Natural shade 60

For the decoration:
Twilleys Goldfingering (80% viscose, 20% polyester, approx. 100m/109yds per 25g/⅞oz ball) 4 ply (fingering) weight yarn
  Small amount of Antique Gold shade 004

4mm (US size G/6) crochet hook

Yarn needle

Polyester toy filling

FINISHED MEASUREMENTS:
7.5cm (3in) diameter

TENSION (GAUGE):
Rounds 1–2 = 4.5cm (1¾in) diameter, using 4mm (US size G/8) hook.

ABBREVIATIONS:
See page 127.

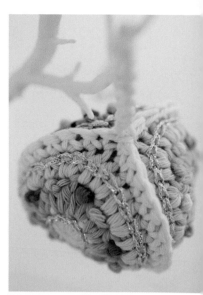

FOR THE BAUBLES

CIRCLE (make 3 for each bauble)

Using first colour, make a magic ring, or ch6 and join with ss in first ch to form a ring.

Round 1: Ch2 (counts as first htr throughout), 9htr into the ring, join with ss in 2nd of beg 2-ch. *10 sts.*
Fasten off first colour.

Round 2: Join second colour in any st, ch2, 1htr in same st, 2htr in each st to end, join with ss in 2nd of first 2-ch. *20 sts.*
Fasten off second colour.

Round 3: Join third colour in any st, ch2, 2htr in next st, *1htr in next st, 2htr in next st; rep from * to end, join with ss in 2nd of first 2-ch. *30 sts.*
Fasten off third colour.

MAKING UP AND FINISHING

JOIN THE CIRCLES

Using any colour and with WS tog, join yarn in any st and join 2 circles with a double crochet seam (see page 124) through the first 15 sts. Take a third circle and begin to join this to the first circle with a double crochet seam. You'll now have one circle joined to half of each of the other two. Stuff with toy filling and then continue working the double crochet seam around to close the opening. Do not fasten off, ch15, and join with a ss in the first chain to make loop to hang the bauble. Fasten off.

Sew in all yarn ends carefully.

ADD DECORATION

Using the gold yarn, work surface crochet (see page 126) around rounds 1 and 3.

Using a contrast colour yarn, work surface crochet around round 2. Alternatively, using two contrasting colours alternately, make French knots (see page 123) into every other st around round 2.

techniques

In this section, we explain how to master the simple crochet and finishing techniques that you need to make the projects in this book.

Holding the hook

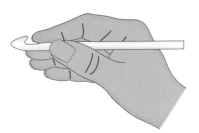

Pick up your hook as though you are picking up a pen or pencil. Keeping the hook held loosely between your fingers and thumb, turn your hand so that the palm is facing up and the hook is balanced in your hand and resting in the space between your index finger and your thumb.

You can also hold the hook like a knife – this may be easier if you are working with a large hook or with chunky yarn. Choose the method that you find most comfortable.

Holding the yarn

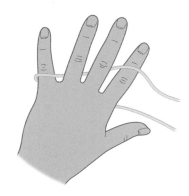 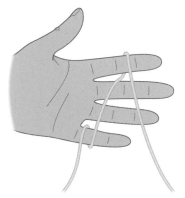

1 Pick up the yarn with your little finger in the opposite hand to your hook, with your palm facing upward and with the short end in front. Turn your hand to face downward, with the yarn on top of your index finger and under the other two fingers and wrapped right around the little finger, as shown above.

2 Turn your hand to face you, ready to hold the work in your middle finger and thumb. Keeping your index finger only at a slight curve, hold the work or the slip knot using the same hand, between your middle finger and your thumb and just below the crochet hook and loop/s on the hook.

Making a slip knot

The simplest way is to make a circle with the yarn, so that the loop is facing downward.

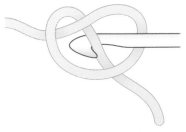 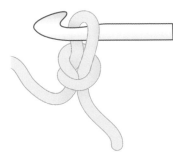

1 In one hand hold the circle at the top where the yarn crosses, and let the end drop down at the back so that it falls across the centre of the loop. With your free hand or the tip of a crochet hook, pull a loop through the circle.

2 Put the hook into the loop and pull gently so that it forms a loose loop on the hook.

Yarn round hook (yrh)

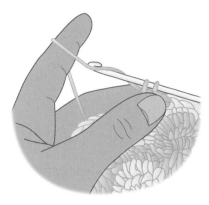

To create a stitch, catch the yarn from behind with the hook pointing upward. As you gently pull the yarn through the loop on the hook, turn the hook so it faces downward and slide the yarn through the loop. The loop on the hook should be kept loose enough for the hook to slide through easily.

Magic ring

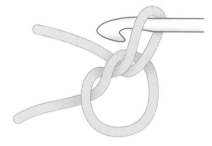

This is a useful starting technique if you do not want a visible hole in the centre of your round. Loop the yarn around your finger, insert the hook through the ring, yarn round hook, pull through the ring to make the first chain. Work the number of stitches required into the ring and then pull the end to tighten the centre ring and close the hole.

Chain (ch)

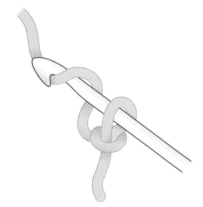

1 Using the hook, wrap the yarn round the hook ready to pull it through the loop on the hook.

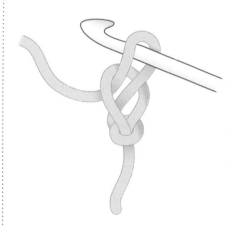

2 Pull through, creating a new loop on the hook. Continue in this way to create a chain of the required length.

Chain ring

If you are crocheting a round shape, one way of starting off is by crocheting a number of chains following the instructions in your pattern, and then joining them into a circle.

1 To join the chain into a circle, insert the crochet hook into the first chain that you made (not into the slip knot), yarn round hook.

2 Pull the yarn through the chain and through the loop on your hook at the same time, thereby creating a slip stitch and forming a circle. You now have a chain ring ready to work stitches into as instructed in the pattern.

Chain space (ch sp)

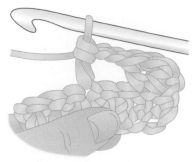

1 A chain space is the space that has been made under a chain in the previous round or row, and falls in between other stitches.

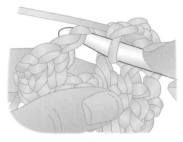

2 Stitches into a chain space are made directly into the hole created under the chain and not into the chain stitches themselves.

Slip stitch (ss)

A slip stitch doesn't create any height and is often used as the last stitch to create a smooth and even round or row.

1 To make a slip stitch: first put the hook through the work, yarn round hook.

2 Pull the yarn through both the work and through the loop on the hook at the same time, so you will have 1 loop on the hook.

Making rounds

When working in rounds the work is not turned, so you are always working from one side. Depending on the pattern you are working, a 'round' can be square. Start each round by making one or more chains to create the height you need for the stitch you are working:
Double crochet = 1 chain
Half treble crochet = 2 chains
Treble crochet = 3 chains
Double treble = 4 chains
Work the required stitches to complete the round. At the end of the round, slip stitch into the top of the chain to close the round.

If you work in a spiral you do not need a turning chain. After completing the base ring, place a stitch marker in the first stitch and then continue to crochet around. When you have made a round and reached the point where the stitch marker is, work this stitch, take out the stitch marker from the previous round and put it back into the first stitch of the new round. A safety pin or piece of yarn in a contrasting colour makes a good stitch marker.

Making rows

When making straight rows you turn the work at the end of each row and make a turning chain to create the height you need for the stitch you are working with, as for making rounds.
Double crochet = 1 chain
Half treble crochet = 2 chains
Treble crochet = 3 chains
Double treble = 4 chains

Working into top of stitch

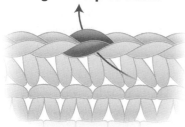

Unless otherwise directed, always insert the hook under both of the two loops on top of the stitch – this is the standard technique.

Working into front loop of stitch (FLO)

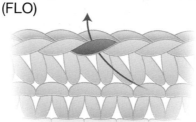

To work into the front loop of a stitch, pick up the front loop from underneath at the front of the work.

Working into back loop of stitch (BLO)

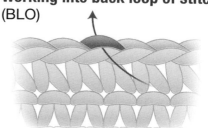

To work into the back loop of the stitch, insert the hook between the front and the back loop, picking up the back loop from the front of the work.

How to measure a tension (gauge) square

Using the hook and the yarn recommended in the pattern, make a number of chains to measure approximately 15cm (6in). Working in the stitch pattern given for the tension (gauge) measurements, work enough rows to form a square. Fasten off. Take a ruler, place it horizontally across the square and, using pins, mark a 10cm (4in) area. Repeat vertically to form a 10cm (4in) square on the fabric. Count the number of stitches across, and the number of rows within the square, and compare against the tension (gauge) given in the pattern.

If your numbers match the pattern then use this size hook and yarn for your project. If you have more stitches, then your tension (gauge) is tighter than recommended and you need to use a larger hook. If you have fewer stitches, then your tension (gauge) is looser and you will need a smaller hook.
Make tension (gauge) squares using different size hooks until you have matched that given in the pattern, and use this hook to make the project.

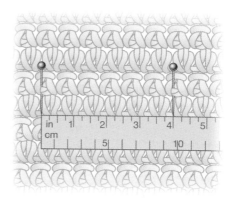

Double crochet (dc)

1 Insert the hook into your work, yarn round hook and pull the yarn through the work only. You will then have 2 loops on the hook.

2 Yarn round hook again and pull through the two loops on the hook. You will then have 1 loop on the hook.

Half treble crochet (htr)

1 Before inserting the hook into the work, wrap the yarn round the hook and put the hook through the work with the yarn wrapped around.

2 Yarn round hook again and pull through the first loop on the hook. You now have 3 loops on the hook.

3 Yarn round hook and pull the yarn through all 3 loops. You will be left with 1 loop on the hook.

Treble crochet (tr)

1 Before inserting the hook into the work, wrap the yarn round the hook. Put the hook through the work with the yarn wrapped around, yarn round hook again and pull through the first loop on the hook. You now have 3 loops on the hook.

2 Yarn round hook again, pull the yarn through the first 2 loops on the hook. You now have 2 loops on the hook.

3 Pull the yarn through 2 loops again. You will be left with 1 loop on the hook.

Double treble (dtr)

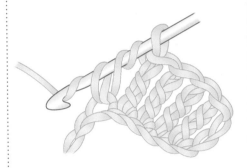

Yarn round hook twice, insert the hook into the stitch, yarn round hook, pull a loop through (4 loops on hook), yarn round hook, pull the yarn through 2 stitches (3 loops on hook), yarn round hook, pull a loop through the next 2 stitches (2 loops on hook), yarn round hook, pull a loop through the last 2 stitches. You will be left with 1 loop on the hook.

Triple treble (ttr)

Triple trebles are 'tall' stitches and are an extension on the basic treble stitch. They need a turning chain of 5 chains.

1 Yarn round hook three times, insert the hook into the stitch or space. Yarn round hook, pull the yarn through the work (5 loops on hook).

2 Yarn round hook, pull the yarn through the first 2 loops on the hook (4 loops on hook).

3 Yarn round hook, pull the yarn through the first 2 loops on the hook (3 loops on hook).

4 Yarn round hook, pull the yarn through the first 2 loops on the hook (2 loops on hook). Yarn round hook, pull the yarn through the 2 loops on the hook. You will be left with 1 loop on the hook.

Elongated double crochet (edc)

This stitch is also sometimes called long double crochet or spike stitch. You just work an ordinary double crochet stitch, but into the stitch that's one, two or more rows below, which creates a V of yarn on the surface. These instructions are for an edc worked into the top of the stitch 2 rows below.

1 Using a contrast yarn, insert your hook into the space one row below the next stitch – this is the top of the stitch one row below, so the same place that the stitch in the previous row is worked.

2 Yarn round hook and draw a loop up so it's level with the original loop on your hook.

3 Yarn round hook and pull through both loops to complete the elongated double crochet.

Front post treble (FPtr)

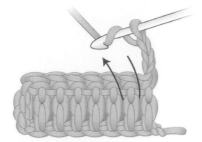

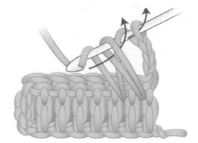

1 Yarn round hook and insert the hook from the front and around the post (the stem) of the next treble from right to left.

2 Yarn round hook and pull the yarn through the work, yarn round hook and pull the yarn through the first 2 loops on the hook.

3 Yarn round hook and pull the yarn through the 2 loops on the hook (1 loop on hook). One front post treble completed.

Back post treble (BPtr)

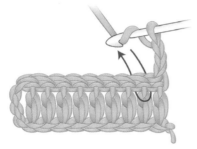

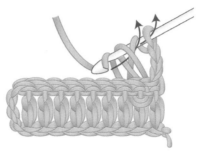

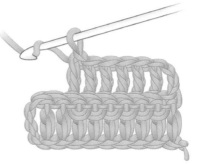

1 Yarn round hook and insert the hook from the back and around the post (the stem) of the next treble as directed in the pattern from right to left.

2 Yarn round hook and pull the yarn through the work, yarn round hook and pull the yarn through the first 2 loops on the hook.

3 Yarn round hook and pull the yarn through the 2 loops on the hook (1 loop on hook). One back post treble completed.

Popcorn stitch (PC)

This example shows a popcorn made with four treble stitches worked into a foundation chain, but a popcorn can be worked into any stitch or space and can be made up of any practical number or combination of stitches.

1 Inserting the hook in the same place each time, work four complete trebles.

2 Slip the hook out of the last loop and insert it into the top of the first stitch.

3 Then insert the hook into the loop of the last stitch again. Yarn round hook and pull it through as indicated.

4 This makes one complete popcorn.

Clusters (cl)

Clusters are groups of stitches, with each stitch only partly worked and then all joined at the end to form one stitch that creates a particular pattern and shape. They are most effective when made using a longer stitch such as a treble. Shown here is a three-treble cluster, but for four- or five-treble clusters, simply repeat steps 1 and 2 more times.

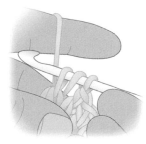

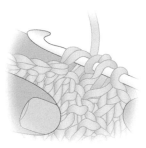

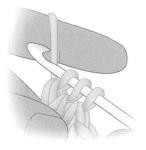

1 Yarn round hook, insert the hook in the stitch (or space). Yarn round hook, pull the yarn through the work (3 loops on hook).

2 Yarn round hook, pull the yarn through 2 of the loops on the hook. Yarn round hook, insert the hook in the same stitch (or space).

3 Yarn round hook, pull the yarn through the work (4 loops on hook). Yarn round hook, pull the yarn through 2 of the loops on the hook (3 loops on hook).

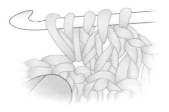

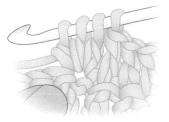

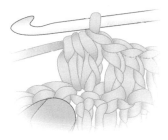

4 Yarn round hook, insert the hook in the same stitch (or space), yarn round hook, pull the yarn through the work (5 loops on hook).

5 Yarn round hook, pull the yarn through 2 of the loops on the hook (4 loops on hook).

6 Yarn round hook, pull the yarn through all 4 loops on the hook (1 loop left on hook). One three-treble cluster made.

Puff stitch (PS)

A puff stitch is a padded stitch worked by creating several loops on the hook before completing the stitch. The basic principle is always the same, but you can repeat steps 1 and 2 fewer times to make a smaller puff. Sometimes a chain is worked at the end to secure the puff.

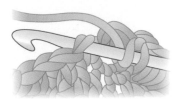

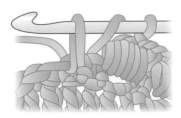

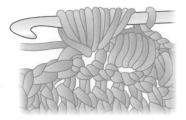

1 Yarn round hook, and insert the hook into the next stitch or space.

2 Yarn round hook again and draw through, keeping the loops of yarn long.

3 Repeat steps 1 and 2 five more times, keeping the loops long each time. There will be 13 loops on the hook.

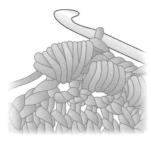

4 Yarn round hook and draw through all the loops on the hook.

5 Yarn round hook, and draw through the single loop on the hook to make a chain and secure the puff stitch.

Increasing

Make two or three stitches into one stitch or space from the previous row. The illustration shows a treble crochet increase being made.

Decreasing

You can decrease by either missing the next stitch and continuing to crochet, or by crocheting two or more stitches together. The basic technique for crocheting stitches together is the same, no matter which stitch you are using. The following example shows dc2tog.

DOUBLE CROCHET TWO STITCHES TOGETHER (dc2tog)

1 Insert the hook into your work, yarn round hook and pull the yarn through the work (2 loops on hook). Insert the hook in next stitch, yarn round hook and pull the yarn through.

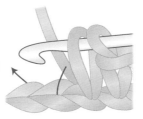

2 Yarn round hook again and pull through all 3 loops on the hook. You will then have 1 loop on the hook.

Joining yarn at the end of a row or round

You can use this technique when changing colour, or when joining in a new ball of yarn as one runs out.

1 Keep the loop of the old yarn on the hook. Drop the end and catch a loop of the strand of the new yarn with the crochet hook.

2 Draw the new yarn through the loop on the hook, keeping the old loop drawn tight and continue as instructed in the pattern.

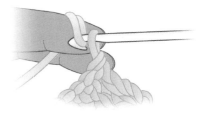

Joining in new yarn after fastening off

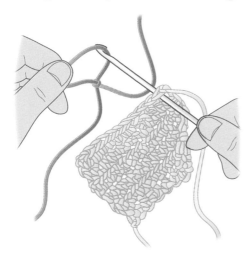

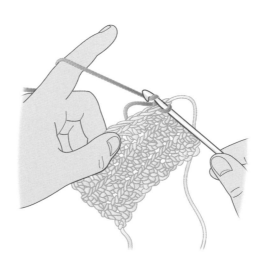

1 Fasten off the old colour (see page 123). Make a slip knot with the new colour (see page 112). Insert the hook into the stitch at the beginning of the next row, then through the slip knot.

2 Draw the loop of the slip knot through to the front of the work. Carry on working using the new colour, following the instructions in the pattern.

Joining yarn in the middle of a row or round

For a neat colour join in the middle of a row or round, use these methods.

JOINING A NEW COLOUR INTO DOUBLE CROCHET

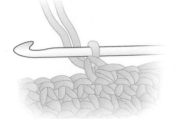 

1 Make a double crochet stitch (see page 115), but do not draw the final loop through, so there are 2 loops on the hook. Drop the old yarn, catch the new yarn with the hook and draw it through both loops to complete the stitch and join in the new colour at the same time.

2 Continue to crochet with the new yarn. Cut the old yarn leaving a 15cm (6in) end and weave the end in (see right) after working a row, or once the work is complete.

JOINING A NEW COLOUR INTO TREBLE CROCHET

1 Make a treble crochet stitch (see page 116), but do not draw the final loop through, so there are 2 loops on the hook. Drop the old yarn, catch the new yarn with the hook and draw it through both loops to complete the stitch and join in the new colour at the same time.

2 Continue to crochet with the new yarn. Cut the old yarn leaving a 15cm (6in) end and weave the end in (see right) after working a row, or once the work is complete.

Join-as-you-go method

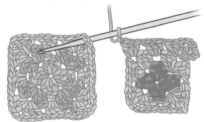 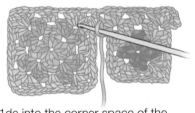 

1 Work the first side of the current square including the first corner grouping (first set of 3htr or 3tr), then instead of making ch2 for the corner space, insert the hook into the corner space of the starting square from underneath as shown.

2 1dc into the corner space of the starting square (counts as first of 2-ch for the corner space), ch1, then work the second 3htr or 3tr grouping into the corner space of the current square as usual.

3 To continue joining the squares together, instead of ch1, work 1dc into the next side space of the starting square.

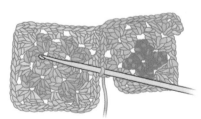 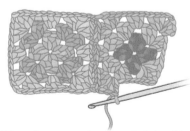 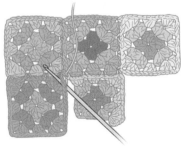

4 Work 3htr or 3tr in the next side space of the current square. Continue replacing each ch-1 at the sides of the current square with 1dc into the next side space of the starting square, and replacing the first of the ch-2 at the corner space of the current square with 1dc into the corner space of the starting square.

5 When the current square is joined to the starting square along one side, continue around and finish the final round of the current square as normal.

6 When joining a current square to two previous squares, replace both corner ch of the current square with 1dc into each adjoining square.

Enclosing a yarn end

You may find that the yarn end gets in the way as you work; you can enclose this into the stitches as you go by placing the end at the back as you wrap the yarn. This also saves having to sew this yarn end in later.

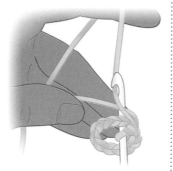

Fastening off

When you have finished crocheting, you need to fasten off the stitches to stop all your work unravelling.

1 Draw up the final loop of the last stitch to make it bigger. Cut the yarn, leaving an end of approximately 10cm (4in) – unless a longer end is needed for sewing up. Pull the end all the way through the loop and pull the loop up tightly.

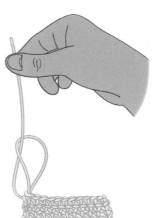

Weaving in yarn ends

It is important to weave in the ends of the yarn so that they are secure and your crochet won't unravel. Thread a yarn needle with the yarn end. On the wrong side, take the needle through the crochet one stitch down on the edge, then take it through the stitches, working in a gentle zig-zag. Work through four or five stitches then return in the opposite direction. Remove the needle, pull the crochet gently to stretch it and trim the end.

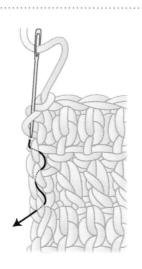

Making a French knot

Bring the needle up from the back of the fabric to the front. Wrap the thread two or three times around the tip of the needle, then reinsert the needle at the point where it first emerged, holding the wrapped threads with the thumbnail of your non-stitching hand, and pull the needle all the way through. The wraps will form a knot on the surface of the fabric.

Blocking

When making some of the projects, such as garlands or mandalas, you will find that taking the time to block and stiffen each crochet element will make a huge difference to the finished effect of your work. Without either of these processes you will find that the crochet will curl out of shape and lose its definition.

For a quick and easy way to block your crochet you'll need blocking pins, some soft foam mats (such as the ones sold as children's play mats) and some ironing spray starch. Pin each item out to shape and size onto the mats and then spray with the starch. Allow to dry for a day before attaching the elements to your garland or mandala.

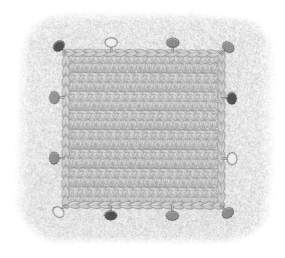

Making an oversewn seam

An oversewn join gives a nice flat seam and is the simplest and most common joining technique.

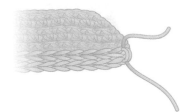

1 Thread a yarn sewing needle with the yarn you're using in the project. Place the pieces to be joined with right sides together.

2 Insert the needle in one corner in the top loops of the stitches of both pieces and pull up the yarn, leaving an end of about 5cm (2in). Go into the same place with the needle and pull up the yarn again; repeat two or three times to secure the yarn at the start of the seam.

3 Join the pieces together by taking the needle through the loops at the top of the corresponding stitches on each piece to the end. Fasten off the yarn at the end, as in step 2.

Making a double crochet seam

With a double crochet seam you join two pieces together using a crochet hook and working a double crochet stitch through both pieces, instead of sewing them together with a yarn end and a yarn sewing needle. This makes a quick and strong seam and gives a slightly raised finish to the edging. For a less raised seam, follow the same basic technique, but work each stitch in slip stitch rather than double crochet.

1 Start by lining up the two pieces with wrong sides together. Insert the hook in the top 2 loops of the stitch of the first piece, then into the corresponding stitch on the second piece.

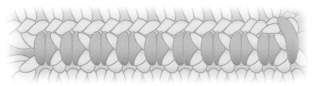

2 Complete the double crochet stitch as normal and continue on the next stitches as directed in the pattern. This gives a raised effect if the double crochet stitches are made on the right side of the work.

3 You can work with the wrong side of the work facing (with the pieces right side facing) if you don't want this effect and it still creates a good strong join.

Sewing up with whip stitch

Whip stitch is an easy way to join pieces, but you will be able to see the stitches clearly, so use a matching yarn. Lay the two pieces to be joined next to each other with right sides facing upward. Secure the yarn to one piece. Insert the needle into the front of the fabric, then up from the back of the adjoining fabric. Repeat along the seam.

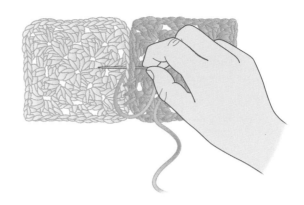

Making pompoms

1 Using a pair of card rings cut to the size of the pompom you would like to create, cut a length of yarn and wind it around the rings until the hole in the centre is filled.

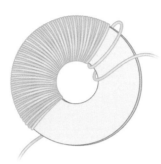

2 Cut through the loops around the outer edge of the rings and ease them slightly apart. Thread a length of yarn between the layers of card and tie tightly, leaving a long end. Remove the card rings and fluff up the pompom. The long yarn end can be used to sew the pompom in place.

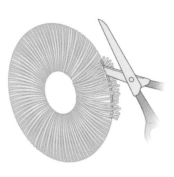

Making tassels

1 Cut yarn to quantity and length given in the pattern. Take suggested bundle of strands and fold in half. With right side of project facing, insert a crochet hook from the wrong side through one of the edge stitches. Catch the bunch of strands with the hook at the fold point.

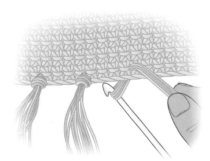

2 Pull the strands on the hook through to make a loop at the back of the work.

3 With your fingers, make the loop bigger and then pull the ends of the bunch of strands through the loop.

4 Pull on the ends to tighten the loop firmly, and secure the tassel.

Surface crochet

Surface crochet is a simple way to add extra decoration to a finished item, working slip stitches over the surface of the fabric.

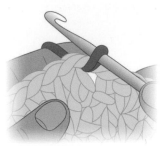 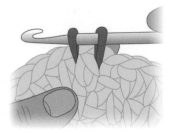 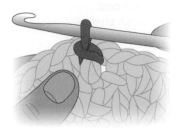

1 Using a contrast yarn, make a slip knot. Holding the yarn with the slip knot behind the work and the hook in front, insert the hook between two stitches from front to the back and catch the slip knot behind the work with the hook. Draw the slip knot back through, so there is 1 loop on the hook at the front of the work.

2 Insert the hook between the next 2 stitches, yarn round hook and draw a loop through to the front. You will now have 2 loops on the hook.

3 Pull the first loop on the hook through the second loop to complete the first slip stitch on the surface of the work.

Repeat steps 2 and 3 to make the next slip stitch. To join two ends with an invisible join, cut the yarn and thread onto a yarn needle. Insert the needle up through the last stitch, into the first stitch as if you were crocheting it, then into the back loop of the previous stitch. Fasten off on the wrong side.

Beading

When using beads, they must all be threaded onto the yarn before you start crocheting. Beads are placed when working with the wrong side of the work facing you. The beads will sit at the back of the work, and so appear on the front (right side).

1 When a bead is needed, slide it up the strand toward the back of the work so it's ready to place in the right part of the stitch you are working.

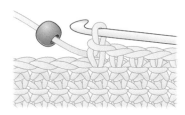

2 Work the stitch as indicated in the pattern. This will secure the bead at the back.

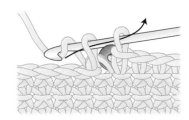

CROCHET STITCH CONVERSION CHART

Crochet stitches are worked in the same way in both the UK and the USA, but the stitch names are not the same and identical names are used for different stitches. Below is a list of the UK terms used in this book, and the equivalent US terms.

UK TERM	US TERM
double crochet (dc)	single crochet (sc)
half treble (htr)	half double crochet (hdc)
treble (tr)	double crochet (dc)
double treble (dtr)	treble (tr)
triple treble (trtr)	double treble (dtr)
quadruple treble (qtr)	triple treble (ttr)
tension	gauge
yarn round hook (yrh)	yarn over hook (yo)

abbreviations

alt	alternat(e)ing
approx.	approximately
beg	begin(ning)
BLO	back loop only
BP	back post
cm	centimetre(s)
cont	continu(e)ing
ch	chain
dc	double crochet
dc2tog	double crochet 2 stitches together
dec	decreas(e)ing
dtr	double treble
edc	elongated double crochet
FLO	front loop only
foll	follow(s)ing
FP	front post
g	gram(mes)
htr	half treble
in	inch(es)
inc	increas(e)ing
m	metre(s)
mm	millimetre(s)
oz	ounce(s)
PM	place marker
patt	pattern
prev	previous
rem	remaining
rep	repeat
RS	right side
ss	slip stitch
st(s)	stitch(es)
sp	space
tog	together
tr	treble
ttr	triple treble
yds	yards
WS	wrong side
yrh	yarn round hook
[ ]	work section between square brackets number of times stated
*	asterisk indicates beginning of repeated section of pattern

suppliers

For reasons of space we cannot cover all stockists, so please explore the local yarn shops and online stores in your own country.

UK

Love Crochet
Online sales
www.lovecrochet.com

Wool
Yarn, hooks
Store in Bath.
+44 (0)1225 469144
www.woolbath.co.uk

VV Rouleaux
Ribbons
Stores in London and Bath, UK.
+44 (0)1225 618600
www.vvrouleaux.com

Deramores
Online sales
www.deramores.com

Laughing Hens
Online sales
Tel: +44 (0) 1829 740903
www.laughinghens.com

John Lewis
Yarns and craft supplies
Telephone numbers of stores on website
www.johnlewis.com

Hobbycraft
www.hobbycraft.co.uk

USA

Knitting Fever Inc.
www.knittingfever.com

WEBS
www.yarn.com

Jo-Ann Fabric and Craft Stores
Yarns and craft supplies
www.joann.com

Michaels
Craft supplies
www.michaels.com

AUSTRALIA

Black Sheep Wool 'n' Wares
Retail store and online
Tel: +61 (0)2 6779 1196
www.blacksheepwool.com.au

Sun Spun
Retail store only
(Canterbury, Victoria)
Tel: +61 (0)3 9830 1609

YARN COMPANIES

Cascade
Stockist locator on website
www.cascadeyarns.com

DMC
Stockist locator on website
www.dmc.com

Rico Design
Stockist locator on website
www.rico-design.de

Rowan Yarns
Stockist locator on website
www.knitrowan.com

Scheepjes
Stockist locator on website
www.scheepjes.com

Stylecraft
Stockist locator on website
www.stylecraft-yarns.co.uk

If you wish to substitute a different yarn for the one recommended in the pattern, try the **Yarnsub** website for suggestions: www.yarnsub.com

acknowledgements

My thanks to Cindy Richards, Penny Craig, Marie Clayton and the team at CICO books for all your support and to Jemima Bicknell for making me look so professional!
Deepest gratitude to Laura Shipley for igniting the flame. To Michael Armstrong for fanning that flame and being there from the very beginning – your faith and belief in me made all the difference. To my colourful friend Rosie Wilks for her help with the Granny Love Blanket and for making this obsession with yarn seem perfectly normal!

To my 'Crazy Correct Ladies' (you know who you are!) who meet every month to hook and drink coffee. To fellow designer Fran Morgan for untangling the knots and Sara Huntington for giving me a chance.

Thank you also to Mirella Lamarina and Christian Henwood for keeping me healthy with their yoga magic and healing touch.

And to my family for putting up with me and my obsession with crochet, especially my nan who planted the seed.

I am profoundly grateful to Rick who competes with my work for space on the sofa, floor, kitchen table and bed (under and on!). Thank you for your encouragement and tolerance and for pretending to know what I'm talking about when I go full crochet on you!

And lastly to my Instagram friends and fellow crocheters who share their work so generously online… you inspire!

The biggest perk to writing a crochet book (beyond being able to say 'I've written a book don't you know!') is being given access to an abundance of yarns. It's been a complete joy and pleasure to have worked so closely with Rico Design and Sheepjes, who have both been so generous – your colours are magical! Thank you also to Stylecraft for supporting this project.

index

a
abbreviations 127

b
back post treble (BPtr) 118
bags and purses
    Neon Sunburst Colour-Pop
        Bag 29–31
    Prayer Beads Purse
        106–109
Basketweave Lap Blanket
    82–83
beading 126
    Light 'n' Airy Beaded
        Toppers 71–73
    Shisha Mirrored Valance
        16–18
blankets
    Basketweave Lap Blanket
        82–83
    Granny Love Blanket
        74–76
blocking 123
Boho Baskets 60–62
Boho Bunting 24–25
bunting 24–25

c
chain (ch) 113
chain ring 113
chain space (ch sp) 114
Christmas Baubles 110–11
clusters (cl) 119
Colourplay Table Runner
    13–15
Comfort Mittens 55–57
corsage 38–39
cushion cover 43–45

d
decreasing 121
double crochet (dc) 115
double treble (dtr) 116
Drifting Thoughts Corsage
    38–39

e
elongated double crochet
    (edc) 117

f
fastening off 123
Flower Power Desk Tidy
    104–105
Flowers in a Bobbin 102–103
French knot 123
front post treble (FPtr) 118

g
garlands
    Heart Garland 96–98
    Prayer Flag Garland 26–28
    Retro Flower Garland
        86–89
Granny Love Blanket 74–76

h
half treble crochet (htr) 116
hanging decorations
    Boho Bunting 24–25
    Christmas Baubles 110–11
    Happy Flowers Chandelier
        32–35
    see also garlands
Hanging Gardens Plant
    Holder 66–67
Happy Flowers Chandelier
    32–35
Heart Garland 96–98
hook, holding 112

i
increasing 120
Indian Summer Table
    Mandala 68–70

j
joining pieces
    double crochet seam 124
    oversewn seam 124
    sewing up with whip
        stitch 125

k l
Kaleidoscope Mandala
    Mat 77–79
Key Ring Charm 99–101
Light 'n' Airy Beaded
    Toppers 71–73

m
Mad Hatter's Tea Cosy 40–42
magic ring 113
mandalas
    Indian Summer Table
        Mandala 68–70
    Kaleidoscope Mandala
        Mat 77–79
    Light 'n' Airy Beaded
        Toppers 71–73
    Mandala Curtain 10–12
    Mandala in a Hoop 63–65
Meditation Rug 50–51
Mindfulness Cowl 48–49
mittens 55–57

n o
Neon Sunburst Colour-Pop
    Bag 29–31
Openwork Winter Scarf
    46–47

p
Peaceful Cushion Cover
    43–45
place mats, coasters and
    runners
    Colourplay Table Runner
        13–15
    Indian Summer Table
        Mandala 68–70
    Summer Sun Coasters
        90–92
    Texture Place Mats 22–23
Plant Holder 66–67
pompoms 125
popcorn stitch (PC) 118
Prayer Beads Purse 106–109
Prayer Flag Garland 26–28
puff stitch (PS) 120

r
Retro Flower Garland 86–89
Ripple Wrap of Mindful
    Imperfections 52–54
rounds, making 114
rows, making 114
rug 50–51

s
scarves and cowls
    Mindfulness Cowl 48–49
    Openwork Winter Scarf
        46–47
seams
    double crochet seam 124
    oversewn seam 124
Secret Garden Autumn Shawl
    80–81
shawls and wraps
    Ripple Wrap of Mindful
        Imperfections 52–54
    Secret Garden Autumn
        Shawl 80–81
Shisha Mirrored Valance
    16–18
skill levels 6
slip knot 112
slip stitch (ss) 114
Squares and Circles Stool
    Cover 19–21
stitch conversion chart 126
Stool Cover 19–21

storage
    Boho Baskets 60–62
    Flower Power Desk Tidy
        104–105
Stress Ball Key Ring Charm
    99–101
Summer Sun Coasters 90–92
suppliers 127
surface crochet 126

t
tassels 125
tea cosy 40–42
Tea Light Holder Cover 93–95
techniques 112–126
tension (gauge) square 115
Texture Place Mats 22–23
treble crochet (tr) 116
triple treble (ttr) 117

w
whip stitch 125
window treatments
    Mandala Curtain 10–12
    Shisha Mirrored Valance
        16–18
working into back loop of
    stitch (BLO) 115
working into front loop of
    stitch (FLO) 115
working into top of stitch 115

y
yarn
    enclosing yarn end 123
    fastening off 123
    holding 112
    join-as-you-go method 122
    joining at end of row or
        round 121
    joining in middle or row or
        round 122
    joining in new yarn 121
    weaving in yarn ends 123
yarn around hook (yrh) 113